Manahune
A to Z

Alice Love

Sketches by Alice Love
Painting by Lila Thomson
Photographs from Albums of Margaret Ansell and Lila Thomson

Alice Love Publications

ISBN: 979-8-89175-144-6 (sc)
ISBN: 979-8-89175-127-9 (hc)
ISBN: 979-8-89175-145-3 (ebk)

Manahune A to Z

For each person – past, present, and future – who has been a blessing [and been blessed] by a stay at Manahune.

Contents

Thanks

Special thanks to my niece Beth McPherson, for her inspiration; and my husband Ken, for his patience and understanding whilst I have been living in the past.

Also thanks to my son Leigh for his generous assistance with his computer expertise, and to Val and Sue Thomson for their helpful proofreading.

Foreword

Beth said that she would like our generation to write of our experiences whilst growing up at Manahune!

I found a very old, hard-covered, empty journal with inset alphabet on the page edges, and picked up a pencil.

Soon there was at least one entry for most of the letters.

Why not fill in the gaps?

These reminiscences cover the years from 1928 to 1947, when I left Manahune to start my training as a nurse.

Manahune
Glenmark
Drive Waipara

The original 'hogget block' of the Glenmark Estate
Drawn by Mrs A.L. Thomson in 1915 in a
ballot for Government leasehold blocks.

The Thomson Family of Manahune 1928

*Left to right: Lila Cobourg, Alice Florence, Albert Archibald,
Lila Margaret, Walter Richard, Alice Louise*

Afternoon Visitors

Once a month the Vicar and his wife would call and have afternoon tea with us. A formal affair, so the front room was swept and dusted and some nice flowers arranged on the table and mantelpiece.

Mum would have baked; and there would be various goodies, including a beautiful cream sponge. My favourite however, was the plate of thinly sliced bread and butter. The outer crust would be cut from the loaf, and the cut end of the loaf spread fairly thinly with butter. This was then sliced from the loaf wafer-thin, the four crusts cut off, and the slice rolled up and placed on a serving plate. The plate was always piled with bread, as this was very popular. The bonus was a nice pile of crusts, which vanished almost as fast as Mum could slice them.

The food and Mum's best tea service were arranged on the tea wagon, and covered with a fancy throw-over. We also were expected to remain clean and tidy (and polite) for the whole afternoon. Sometimes some of the local ladies would call and receive the same treatment.

At the end of the afternoon, when the guests had been duly escorted down the front steps, along the rose-bordered path to the little wooden gate and their parked cars, there was a rush of children back to the sitting room to help clear the used cups, saucers and plates.

The first thing to receive attention was the plate with the few remaining pieces of bread and butter.

Amberley Pictures

On Saturday evenings one could go to the pictures in the Amberley Town Hall. Occasionally Dad would take the older children while Mum stayed home with the younger ones.

We all stood for *God Save the King*. There would be a newsreel, then an episode of the current serial; sometimes "The Lone Ranger", always finishing with the hero in some hopeless predicament, where he had to remain until the next Saturday.

After a short interval came the feature film. I remember seeing *The Wizard of Oz, Pygmalion* (the precursor to *My Fair Lady*), and a few others. I have memories of covering my eyes to shut out anything too gruesome.

When we arrived home, we poured into the kitchen where Mum was waiting with a large plate of hot buttered toast.

American Marines

In the middle of the war years American Servicemen were in camp at Paraparaumu, for respite between fighting the Japanese in the Pacific. Before they were sent back to the war zone, these lads were billeted out in private homes for a week.

One week, Waipara was asked to take a turn and two nice young boys were billeted at Manahune. One of them had a bad bout of malaria while with us, and spent quite a bit of time shivering uncontrollably in bed. They both spent time each day throwing a tennis ball to each other, practicing returning a grenade, should it be lobbed within catching distance.

A special dance was quickly organised as part of the district entertainment for our American guests.

Left to Right: Roy Loppe, Tom, Margaret, Eddie Fisher, Clarence Backus

Animals Wild

Mice were prolific among the chaff sacks in the woolshed; and when the last layer of sheaves was lifted from an oat stack, they ran in all directions. We always wore gumboots for this purpose and would stamp on as many as possible.

One of the boys caught one and lifted it by the tail. He received a bitten finger for his pains.

In the autumn it was hard to keep mice out of the house, and mousetraps were set in strategic places. The pantry door was always kept shut, but if any mouse gnawed its way in, the hole was quickly discovered and a piece of tin nailed over it.

Rats could be seen sometimes, running along the rafters in the woolshed; and a rat trap was usually set in the dairy. They would help themselves to walnuts in the orchard. A few times a half rat was lying on the lawn in the morning, and one knew that one of the cats had done a good job.

There were a few opossums about, and they made their presence known by sliding down the corrugated iron roof at night.

Hedgehogs were enjoyed, and were probably glad to escape our attentions, and get back to serious business in the garden.

Skink lizards could be found on warm banks and rocks, and were sometimes caught by the cats. The fowl house received a few visits from ferrets. There would be a terrible racket during the night and their trail of carnage could usually be followed to the hole with their young in it. This resulted in some cyanide being placed in the hole, and the entrance was then earthed over.

One cheeky ferret was seen disappearing into a hole under the mandarin tree, right beside the kitchen door. Not the place for cyanide; so a gintrap was baited with a chook the ferret had killed, and was then placed in front of the hole. The ferret was very quickly caught and dispatched with a shotgun. What wasn't so quickly disposed of was the aroma just outside the kitchen door.

Rabbits could be very prolific and were shot if possible. One year a rabbiter came on the property. He had about twenty assorted dogs, including whippets, greyhounds and fox terriers. That reduced the rabbit population for a while.

Hares were quite plentiful. We attempted to keep the odd small rabbit as a pet, but that was rather frowned upon by the adults. One day they gave us a fat white rabbit with pink eyes. I don't remember its final fate, but we enjoyed having it.

Our most rare visits were from wild deer. A few times one would be sighted on the hills, and one once passed quite close to the house.

Audrey's Twenty-First

On a hot November evening in 1946, Dad took Margaret and me to 7 Washbourne Street, for Audrey's twenty-first birthday party. We had already had a long day in the shearing shed.

A very happy evening was had by all, and over a delicious supper Uncle Leonard asked the age-old question, what is the difference between a weasel and a stoat?

On the way home, in the back of the Austin 7, I had my first nosebleed. It was a cracker!

Leonard and Molly Hamilton

Birds

Magpie

Magpies warbled in the pine trees. Nests were so high that only rarely could we climb to them, and so vigorously defended that it wasn't worth the effort.

During nesting season, it was wise to wear a hat and carry a stick in some areas of the garden to ward off swooping magpies.

Some magpies were good mimics of human voices. One magpie could call the dogs in Dad's voice and Mum had been known to put the kettle on, because she thought Dad was home and would like a cup of tea.

Fledgling magpies are easy to tame and we had a few pets over the years. The very best was Harold's pet. It would get into bed with Harold in the morning.

Sparrow

A flock of sparrows occasionally would harass a magpie and put it to flight.

House sparrows were in large flocks with several nests in most pine trees. It was open season on sparrows' eggs, and every two or three days in the spring we would make the rounds of the nests. I think the only trees we hadn't managed to climb were the poplar by the dog kennels and the blue gum. Dad sometimes paid us for collecting these eggs because the large flocks of sparrows would swoop down when he was feeding the hens and take most of the wheat.

Occasionally, when the numbers got too high, he would resort to poisoning them. He shut the hens away and put out poisoned wheat. It was our job to take a bucket and go around under all the trees and pick up all the dead sparrows. These were duly counted and buried so the cats wouldn't eat them and be poisoned in turn. This would reduce the numbers for a while.

Finally, Dad built a hen yard completely enclosed in bird netting, and he fed the hens in there.

Occasionally the wrong birds would get poisoned, and we would be very sad to be picking up dead goldfinches, as well as sparrows.

One day Margaret and I had five or six dead goldfinches; and when we buried the

Goldfinch

sparrows in the rose garden, we couldn't bear to cover those pretty red and gold heads with dirt, so we planted them with their heads above ground!

Thrush

As well as our sparrow nesting, we knew where most of the other birds' nests were, and we would make the rounds of these nests too, just to watch progress.

In the orchard and pine hedge would be blackbird, thrush, hedge sparrow, goldfinch and yellow hammer; and round the creek in the matagouri bushes would be the hanging nests of the grey warbler (rainbird); we were also lucky enough to find skylarks' nests in the grass along roadsides, and on pasture land too.

Blackbird

At that time there were lots of skylarks, and one could usually hear them singing on a fine day and see them spiraling high above.

Starlings nested around the woolshed, and an odd wild duck in the swamp. Sometimes at harvest time a hawk's nest on the ground would be disturbed. Other birds visited, but I didn't see their nests – moreporks, fantails, woodpigeons, pukekos, paradise

Skylark

ducks, shining cuckoo, greenfinch, chaffinch and kingfisher, and there were several visits to the orchard by a kaka.

One day Margaret and I found the kaka in a fairly low plum tree and tried to catch it. Alas, the tail feathers came away in one's hand!

We had damaged a *Kaka*
Kakas were *Protected*
There was *Evidence*
There would be *Penalties*

Kaka

Did anyone ever wonder how a handful of green feathers came to be in an old cow's skull at the back of the orchard?

Another day, Margaret found some old hairy brown feathers not far from the creek flat campsite. Dad identified them as weka.

Wekas were plentiful in the swamp before 1920. They would abscond with a hot mutton chop from the frypan; or an unguarded boot from beside the tent and disappear among the nigger-heads into the swamp.

Left: Weka
Right: Pukeko

White leghorn chooks supplied our eggs and, later, enough eggs to take weekly to the Egg Floor in Bedford Row, behind the Farmers in Christchurch.

During wartime egg rationing, all eggs had to be sold through the Egg Floor. The eggs were collected and washed, and packed into crates in the scullery, and Dad would take them into town on the back of the Austin 7. At the peak of this business every egg was stamped Guaranteed Fresh TB [for Thomson Bros].

Initially they would buy six-week-old pullets, but when it became more of a business, it was day-old chicks, which would arrive on the train from Buttons in Rose Street, Spreydon.

Dad met the train and brought home several boxes with holes punched at intervals all over the sides and tops. Each box contained fifty chickens and now it was all go.

Mum had prepared wooden nursery boxes lined with old woollen material and with strips of material hanging down from the lids, so that the chicks would be snug and warm. In the bottom there was newspaper and a layer of chaff.

The dining facilities consisted of an open-topped box with newspaper on the floor. Drinking dishes were porridge plates, with an upturned preserving jar of water in the middle that self-fed as the water level lowered. Mum mixed up a brew of chopped hard-boiled egg and oatmeal, and later this had finely chopped silver beet added to it, and then kibbled wheat.

Where was this nursery set up? In the kitchen, of course, along the west wall. After a few days the boxes would be outside on fine days, and the sleeping boxes migrated to the scullery over night.

I think the next step was chicken coops on the lawn until they were old enough to join the hens.

In tandem with the poultry business was a flock of Indian Runner ducks. They were fed with the hens by the gate into the yard, and then did their own thing with regards to spending the day on the creek; and nesting and hatching their young. The eels in the creek were taking most of the ducklings. So Plan B was to build a duck house and run at the back of the orchard, and as each brood hatched, they were collected and put in the duck house with a few mother ducks.

For a few years I was responsible for the ducks, and would mix up buckets of pollard for the young ones. I loved the baby ducklings and still prefer them to chickens. When they were old enough to be safe from the eels, they were set free to join the adults again.

We used duck eggs for cooking and some of the family liked the slightly stronger taste as a poached egg.

The ducks, like the hens, could become a family dinner. Once I was asked to behead a duck for this purpose. I caught the duck, carried it to the chopping block and picked up the axe. The duck turned its head and looked at me…

That duck was safe, and I never brought myself to attempt that feat again.

Walter and Dorothy introduced turkeys to the farm, and apart from keeping out of the way of the gobblers, I found them mildly interesting. They made a very nice dinner!

Books

Dad would read the newspaper each day and knew his Bible very well. Mum had always loved reading, but for many years she just didn't have enough time to indulge this passion.

Dad's dictionary would be used several times a week. Over the years he wore out more than one.

We started with cloth books when very tiny, and progressed through cardboard models to picture books, to good storybooks.

Margaret Sansom gave us books for birthdays and Christmas, and finally she gave us the books she had as a girl, as well as a set of Junior Encyclopaedia.

My appetite for reading was insatiable, and I had soon read all the children's books on our long bookshelf. There was a bookcase full of assorted books in the sitting room; and that was my next ambition – to read them all. I had done so before I was eleven, including Dad's veterinary book and the Bible. Some of the books were of doubtful suitability for a ten-year-old.

If I hadn't appeared in the cowshed at milking time, I was probably lying on my bed, reading.

Grannie Fendall spent most of her time reading in her last few years. She once told me, "This book is just for Grannies." Of course I had to find out why, as soon as possible, but not anywhere near my Grannie!

Buttercups

As one descends the hill towards the Kowhai River bridge at Leithfield, on the left is a little dell. Sometimes this is golden with buttercups. Dad was ecstatic whenever he saw them.

Cats

Cats are part of the working team on a farm, with the brief to keep the mouse and rat population at a reasonable level and vary their diet with the odd rabbit or bird.

One or two learned the art of fishing, and could be seen at the creek waiting for a suitable sized eel to come within reach. It would be quickly flicked out of the water and seized around the neck. When dead it would be dragged up the hill, and proudly displayed before being eaten.

A row of cats would appear at the cowshed at milking time and wait hopefully for a well directed squirt of milk—straight from cow to cat. The first of the skim milk from the separator filled a dish for the cats and was quickly surrounded. Kittens of course were an annual event, and it was necessary to keep the numbers to a reasonable level.

Harold with Little Black One

One year there were twenty-three assorted cats, and dire threats from Dad. A multi-coloured carpet of cats lay in the sun outside the scullery door, and appeared to just commute from there to the cowshed.

A certain amount of night time caterwauling was to be heard, especially in the spring.

One cat later perfected the art of catching birds. She would sit on the kitchen roof, watching and assessing; when she finally launched herself, she would catch the bird in flight and land on the ground, bird in mouth.

Church

Mum and Dad would take all of us to church each month for the Communion Service, and occasionally we would go to other services as well. Later, our family was on the roster for cleaning the church and doing the flowers.

The Glenmark Church, from a painting by Lila Thomson

We would turn up in the Austin 7 complete with vacuum cleaner, dusters and a bucket with a little water in it and lots of flowers.

The wee Austin 7 was small enough to be driven through the lychgate, which then was on the main road below the east end of the church, and up the winding path, right to the church door.

All the parishioners would turn out to decorate the church for Harvest Thanksgiving, and Manahune grapes were always a part of the decoration.

On occasions like this we were able to look behind the organ where, originally, a lad would work the bellows; and we would climb up to the belfry, to admire the carillon of bells.

Of course this was very familiar territory for Mum, as her father had been Vicar of Glenmark for five years, until his retirement in the late 1920s.

Mum and Dad were married in the Glenmark Church in January 1926 by her father, the Rev. F.P. Fendall. Dad's brother, Walter, was best man; Mum's cousin Norman, groomsman, and her sister Hilda, and best friend
Margaret Sansom were the bridesmaids.

Walter, Bert, Hilda, Lila, Norman, Margaret

I remember once riding my bicycle to church – a reminder that while Mum and Dad were engaged, she would ride her bicycle from the vicarage to Manahune, on a very rough shingle road with seven fords to cross. Mum was ecstatic about the scent of the white clover along the roadsides, for the rest of her life.

The next Vicar was the Rev. Henry Hawkins, who perfected the mechanism that tied the sheaves on the reaper and binder.

After Mr Hawkins it was the Rev. James Hay. In his tenure of the parish, he established and taught Sunday school in the Waipara School.

Initially Dad would drive us to Sunday school in the Austin 7, and then we started riding horses to Sunday school. One had to arrive early enough to unsaddle the horses and turn them loose in the horse paddock behind the school.

As we rode down the drive we would hear each other's catechism.

When John was old enough to go with us, we upgraded to the spring cart, with Margaret the responsible driver of Prince.

I don't remember much of the Sunday school lessons, with the exception of hearing of each child's catechism! Quite early I had learned the whole thing, and my reward was to learn the Collect for the week (from the prayer book) by heart, and to recite that as well.

Margaret quickly caught on, and it was surprising how long it took her to learn that catechism.

As we drove up the Glenmark Drive on the way home, Ted Whyte would join us on his horse, as he rode up to have Sunday dinner with the Symonds family. Ted was courting Phyllis Symonds.

At the age of twelve or thirteen, I rebelled at going to Sunday school. My argument was that I had already joined the same class as Bert, and if I stayed there any longer I would have progressed to John's class.

Clothes

Because our early years were depression ones, clothes were strictly utility. Not much store was set on fashion or dressing up.

Skirts had a bodice top with a large tuck that could be let down as one grew. The deep bottom hem had the same thought in mind. Over the skirt would be a blouse with elastic waistband and/or a jersey. On top would be a pinny that covered most of the outer garment.

Footwear was simple; often there wasn't any. In winter we wore socks and gumboots and sandals for best. Sometimes, instead of a skirt, we would wear a straight pinafore dress over a blouse.

Underwear was bloomers with elastic waist and legs, and a cotton singlet – plus a woollen one for cooler weather.

Margaret and Alice

Mum made our skirts, blouses, pinafores and nightgowns. She made her own dresses too; using a hand turned sewing machine, which was quite tricky to work, as there was only one hand free to guide the sewing. Later, Dad obtained a sewing table with a treadle attached, and Mum's hand machine was converted to a treadle one. This table had a series of small drawers for cottons and other accessories.

Mum was good at knitting socks, but the men's boots were too hard on them to make it economic. She was very good with a crochet hook and crocheted garments for her babies.

We usually had a best set of outer clothes – Margaret's were often green and mine pink. This colour scheme was repeated when we were flower girls for Walter's and Dorothy's wedding.

Dorothy made each of us long dresses of floral printed organdie with a frill around the hem and puffed sleeves. We wore a string of artificial pearls, and white socks with black patent leather shoes that had a buttoned strap. We had never seen anything so wonderful! Our hair was wrapped with curling rags overnight, to produce ringlets for the occasion. A few parcels of hand-me-downs came our way, and I just loved a pale yellow dress with a smocked waist, that I was able to wear for two years. It was still good enough to pass on again.

At one stage Mum bought us liberty bodices; brushed cotton, close fitting vests that fastened up the front. They should have been warm and comfortable, but I loathed the thought of wearing them, and made such a fuss that Mum gave up in disgust.

In our teens, Margaret and I attended a dressmaking class with Mum. We made ourselves quite reasonable dresses.

Our classmates from Waipara School who had moved on to various secondary schools, now wore gym frocks and blouses with a tie for school uniform. Since we were doing correspondence lessons at home, we acquired gym frocks to wear when we went to town and enjoyed dressing up in them.

Carefully folded away in tissue paper, in a box in the spare room cupboard, was Mum's wedding dress and veil. It was a mid-calf fairly straight dress in 1920s style, but made of beautiful figured satin. The veil was a similar length.

Occasionally we would get them out and duly admire them. When Margaret was married, Joan Quigley made a beautiful job of converting Mum's dress to a long one, with plain satin. Margaret wore this with Mum's veil and looked lovely. A few years later I wore the same outfit for our wedding.

Joan Quigley, Margaret, Alice

Margaret and I both had long hair, which was cut when we started school at Waipara. We both grew it again once we were home and wore it in two plaits crossed at the back and wrapped around our heads. When I started nursing this fashion caught on, and soon a fair number of nurses were wearing their hair this way.

Margaret and Alice

While we attended Waipara School, we wore lace-up shoes and socks and a dress and cardigan. For working on the farm in our teens, the outfit was slacks and blouses.

Bert and Walter Thomson

Formal wear for men included starched white collarless shirts. The shiny, commercially starched, stiff winged collars were attached with a collar stud at the back of the shirt neck. A larger stud went through two layers of shirt neckband, and two layers of collar base at the front neck. A tie was always worn with this.

Trousers were held up with braces, and a waistcoat and jacket completed the picture.

The starched collars were kept in a round leather box to maintain their pristine condition. Collar studs and tiepins had their own container on the dressing table; this contained some mainly unused cufflinks as well.

Work shirts had collars attached, and it was probably the late 1940s before dress shirts had attached collars too.

The well-dressed man always wore a hat outside, and this was doffed when he was introduced to a lady, or on any other occasion necessitating a show of respect; for instance, the passing of a funeral cortage.

The felt fedora was never worn inside; and there were rows of hat pegs in the entrance porches of all halls and churches, and private homes too.

Dad wore a sunhat for work, sometimes straw, but usually a grey cloth hat with a green under-brim lining. A cloth cap graced one of the pegs in the hall, but it didn't get many outings.

Bert Thomson (Dad)

Wet weather gear was oilskins, which hung in a row, on nails, on the internal scullery wall – with rows of gumboots below.

The men used a pocket watch. It would have a hinged cover to protect the glass, and a winding knob at the top. Over the winder was a metal ring to which was attached a watch chain. The chain, in turn was attached to a Waistcoat buttonhole, or to the top of one's working trousers.

Ladies wore the only wristwatches. My Grannie gave me my first watch. It was very dainty with a mother-of-pearl face and I loved it. I was wearing it one day when we were riding horses out on the farm. When we returned the watch was missing and I never did find it again.

Cows

Cows were an integral part of Manahune life. Initially they had been milked on the track outside the little iron gate, handy to the dairy. Rain or shine, the milkers carried a box and a bucket and seated themselves beside an obliging cow. If the cow decided it would be more comfortable a few paces this way or that, the milker had to follow; and always be alert to the placing of a heavy cloven hoof – against the bucket, in the bucket, or even on one's own foot. If the flies were troublesome, a flicking tail was indiscriminate about its target.

When we were introduced to the joys of milking at late three or early four, there was a five bail cowshed with four of the bails under cover.

The boxes now sported a folded sack for comfort; and there was also a leg rope, plus a four-inch nail driven into the post on the cow's offside, on which the matted end of a flicking tail could be immobilized.

Between eighteen and twenty cows were being hand-milked twice daily in those days.

Margaret and Alice

There was an enclosed raceway from near the house gate, to a holding yard past the cowshed, with a gate either end of the race, and another into the holding yard.

Some of the cows had a preference for which bail they were in; and also in which order they were milked. We also had our favourite cows, and would hurry to finish milking one cow, so we could choose which cow we milked next.

Usually on the walk to the cowshed, the cows had emptied bladders and bowels, but standing in the yard waiting their turn could alter that situation.

It was usual to occasionally make them all change position [stir up the cows] before the bails were refilled. Even so, it was necessary to be on the alert for a rising tail: as the spatters could catch the milker or, worse still, the bucket. At the first sign, there was a dash for a shovel, strategically leaning against the middle of the rail fence, opposite the bails. This shovel hopefully caught all the offending material, and was emptied over the fence into the orchard. If necessary, the concrete was cleared with the shovel and then hosed down.

When one collected the cows for milking, frequently they would cross the creek and come up the hill below the gum tree. It was usual to grab hold of a cow's tail and be helped up the hill. When Harold was quite small, he had the hang of that technique, but was not sufficiently alert. The cow that was towing him let fly with a particularly runny brew, and Harold wore the lot.

The cows were all named and had distinct personalities. There were Shorthorn, Holstein, and Friesian, and crosses of these; also one little Jersey cow named Ruby. Ruby was Walter's pet and she was very jealous of his attention.

When Dorothy came on the scene, she couldn't walk across the yard with Walter when Ruby was about, or a very angry little cow would threaten her.

Usually there was a bull running with the herd and we were very wary of him.

Occasionally a neighbour's bull would pay a visit, and there would be a no-holds-barred bullfight, until they were separated, and the visitor returned to his own domain. During one fight the contestants sparred all the way up the hill track to the top gate into the homestead paddock. Here there was a lull in hostilities while they each caught their breaths. In an unguarded moment, one turned his back and received a prod with a horn that caused a high leap in the air – straight up a vertical bank, and over the top of a five-wire-and barb fence on the top, into the calf paddock. I still find it hard to imagine how he did it!

New calves were separated from their mums early, and were given her milk to drink until it was clear and ready for separating.

The calves were taught how to drink from a bucket by sucking one's fingers under the surface of the milk. They soon caught on. Until they could drink, they were kept in a small pen in the orchard, and then they were put in the calf paddock.

The buckets were of two types; round, tapered milk buckets, or kerosene tins with tops cut out, sharp edges hammered down and a No.8 wire handle inserted.

The full buckets were carried past the house to the concrete-floored dairy under the pine trees. Here the milk was separated; the cream going straight into cream cans that were collected from the mail box area twice a week, and the skim milk carried back and used to feed calves, dogs and pigs. Sometimes there would be a surplus that went into a 44-gallon drum behind the hen house.

Bert, Margaret and John

The separator was hand turned, and each rotation of the handle rang a bell. One could tell by the tone of the ring when it was up to speed.

Initially it was Grandma Thomson's (self appointed) task to do the separating, until she died in 1931. Thereafter, whoever was free would turn the handle.

Once there were enough buckets of milk to keep the separator going, someone would stop milking and take over that job.

One day some buckets of milk en route to the dairy had been set down near the house by the grapevine. At about three years of age, I was busy making mud pies just outside the kitchen door. I noticed this lovely milk and dipped in my muddy tin to get some. It made beautiful mud pies. Later, when Dad went to tip the milk into the separator, he discovered the muddy sediment and traced the culprit. I think that was my first good smack!

When all the milk was separated, a small bottle of water followed, to clear out the last of the milk and cream. Then the various parts of the machine were placed in the large bowl and carried to the scullery, ready for the lucky person whose job it was to wash the separator.

It was dismantled, rinsed with cold water then washed with hot water and washing soda – all parts being cleaned with a brush before being rinsed with clean hot water. Then it was placed on the separator shelf outside the back door, to air.

The various components were: a strainer with a removable gauze base held in with a wire clip. This was covered with a double layer of butter muslin, clipped on with four dolly clothes pegs. The butter muslin was frequently boiled or replaced as necessary.

A homemade frame of four wooden slats supported the strainer over the large milk bowl.

There was a slide-in tapered tap at the base of the milk bowl, which was opened when the separator was up to speed; for washing, the tap was removed and cleaned with a bottlebrush.

The main component of the separator was a bell-shaped metal contraption, made up of a circular base plate that slotted onto the turning mechanism.

The raised outer edge had a slot to let out the skim milk. Up the centre was a hollow pipe, with vertical slots to let the milk through between a series of truncated metal cones with holes in them. They slid down over the centre pipe. A rubber ring inside the base edge formed a seal when a locking ring on top - that was 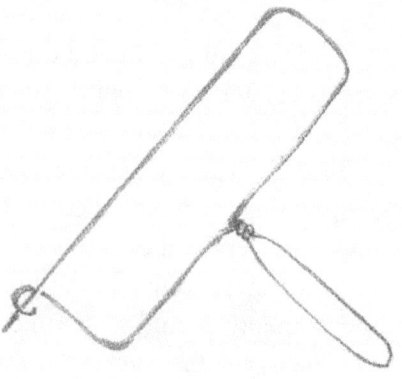 tightened with a special spanner - screwed the outer cover down. Near the top was an adjustable hole to let out the cream. Two spouts sitting one above the other took the cream and milk to their respective containers.

When the separator itself was dismantled, the discs, rubber ring and screw top were slid onto a special wire that allowed them to be moved apart for cleaning, but be kept in the right order for easy re-assembly.

During the mid 1930s a separator house was built on the back of the cowshed, and the long carry of heavy milk buckets was almost eliminated.

The original dairy had a concrete floor with a butter-well set into the front right corner. This well was deep enough to hold a large square biscuit tin for butter; and there was plenty of room for jugs of milk and jars of cream. A wooden lid could be easily lifted off. The butter was kept nicely firm in summer, and we set jellies there too.

There was no electricity on Manahune until late 1938.

The dairy windows were of wire netting. There was a bench full-length on the back wall; and above it a shelf that contained our bottled fruit, over 100 two-litre jars each year. Behind the dairy were wire netting shelves for storing apples, pears and pumpkins over the winter.

Butter was made weekly and the surplus was sold to the grocer. The wooden butter churn sat on the bench in the dairy. Inside it were four wooden beaters attached to the spindle. This could all be dismantled for cleaning.

The cream for churning sat in the dairy for one or two days, but was still sweet.

Prior to churning, the wooden bench in the scullery was scrubbed and scalded; two large pieces of butter muslin and the two butter pats were dipped in boil-

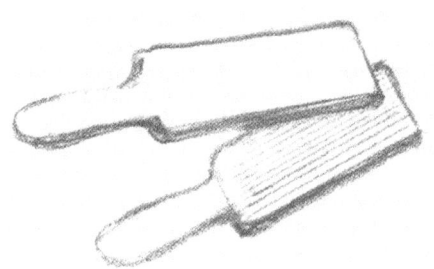

ing water and then cooled. The pats were the length and width of a pound of butter, and one side was smooth and the other side ridged lengthwise. The churn was scalded with boiling water, then rinsed out with cold.

The temperature of the cream was taken with a dairy thermometer; the optimum temperature for churning is 62F (16.7C). In the winter, if the temperature was too low, a little hot water was stirred into the cream.

When the temperature was correct, the cream was poured into the churn to just below the spindle, the wooden lid replaced, and the handle turned until the butter separated from the buttermilk. If the temperature wasn't right, this could be a long job.

The butter would clump together, and the buttermilk could be poured off, and either used in the kitchen or discarded.

The churn, with its load of butter, was carried to the scullery and emptied into the sink. The butter was rinsed under the cold tap and placed on the cold wet bench.

With a folded piece of damp butter muslin in each hand, Mum would now knead and work the butter to remove any pockets of buttermilk. The butter was then sprinkled with a measured amount of salt and kneaded and worked again, to distribute the salt evenly. A much larger amount of salt could have been put in the churn with the cream, but most of it would be lost with the buttermilk, which also would be too salty to use.

The next step was to divide the butter into 1-lb lots, checked by scales, though Mum could judge it very well. Now the butter pats quickly and efficiently shaped the pounds of butter, which could have either smooth or ridged sides, according to which side of the pats was used – a handy way to differentiate between salted and unsalted butter. The shaped pound was placed with the pats squarely in the middle of a pre-cut rectangle of greaseproof paper, which we soon learned to wrap and fold in a professional manner.

The batch of new butter was put in a biscuit tin in the well in the dairy.

The final job was the washing of churn, pats, bench and butter muslin – working on wet wood, helped prevent absorption of the grease, and made the clean up easier.

Dances

Ballroom dancing was very much in vogue during the 1930s and '40s, and dances were the entertainment of choice over the winter months.

During the war years each serviceman was farewelled by the district with a dance in his honour – hopefully there would be another one for him on his return.

Dad took Margaret and me to all of these. In our teens we had some ballroom dancing lessons but most of it we learned on the dance floor.

The criteria for entrance to the hall was, 'Men the appropriate coins and Ladies a plate'. Those plates were well filled and the suppers were delicious.

Usually there was a three-piece band; piano and saxophones; and at times we would dance to the bagpipes.

Occasionally Mum and the boys would attend a dance too.

Dogs

Four or five sheepdogs were a necessity on a sheep farm the size of Manahune.

Initially, a row of kennels beside the pine trees extended northwards from the long drop. Each dog had his own kennel, and by the door a metal standard was driven into the ground, with a loop at the end of the dog chain slipped over it. A water container was placed at a distance where the dog could reach it without entangling it with his chain.

One of the dogs was good with cows so was let off the chain to help with the round up before milking. The rest were let off together when Dad was ready to go out on the farm. There would be much excitement and barking when they saw him coming.

They were well trained and saved a lot of footwork when rounding up or droving sheep. At the end of the day they were again chained up by their kennel.

A small mob of older 'dog tucker' sheep were kept for that purpose; and one would be killed as necessary for maintaining a supply for the dog's daily meals.

The dog kennels were later moved to the base of the row of pine trees at the top of the calf paddock.

At one stage Dad had a bitch among the dogs, but I remember only one litter of pups.

At shearing time, some of the dogs were very good at working the sheep into the shed and penning up. They would run across the backs of the sheep if necessary.

Dragonflies

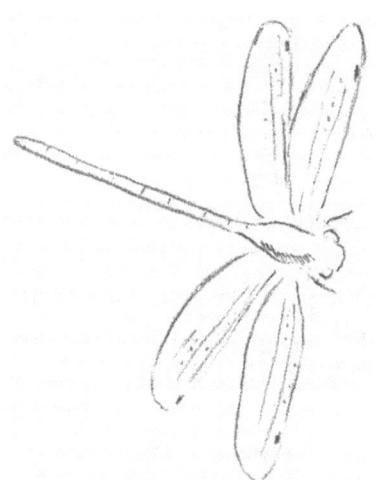

Wherever there was water there were dragonflies, darting and hovering over the creek or resting on a blade of grass.

Two pairs of transparent gauzy wings and a long slim abdomen, attached to a sturdy little thorax with six hairlike legs, their bold colours would shimmer in the summer sun; red, blue, green and black.

A helicopter-like giant dragonfly would sometimes fly across the lawn and gardens, going about his business with a very determined, unstoppable air. We quickly moved out of his way, but I guess he was harmless enough.

Where dragon flies darted, closer inspection would reveal a busy community beneath that slightly rippled surface.

A cockabully or two, resting, then darting and then resting again. A water beetle floating to the surface on a bubble of air and maybe some nymphs and a water spider seeking prey. A small fly lands, and the surface tension gives him secure footing – mind that spider and those bullies!

Education

Dad had wanted to be a doctor but had to leave school early to earn a living. He continued his education throughout his life. He was a very good speller. More than one dictionary was worn out through use over the years. It always sat in a prominent place in the kitchen, and any unfamiliar word was researched and used.

Mum, as a prolific reader, had a strong grasp of grammar and the English language; and we were taught to speak correctly from a very early age. Books were always a part of Manahune life.

Mum's Uncle George had a poetic bent; he even preached a complete sermon in rhyme, and this was something Mum also had inherited.

When either Dad or Mum had heard our prayers and tucked us into bed, it was time to start calling "Oncle Water, Oncle Water."

"What do you want?"

"Tell us a story."

Uncle Walter would always oblige, and bedtime stories ended each day for Margaret and me, and Bert too, as a little chap.

Mum had trained as a midwife, and said she had chosen that branch of nursing because, in general, the patients were well and the outcome was almost always a happy one.

At an early age I had decided I wanted to be a nurse. I had too good an imagination to even consider being a doctor! There were scenarios I didn't even wish to think about!

While I was doing my training, Mr Reeves, who had taught us for several years at Waipara, was one of my patients. The first thing he said to me was, "Why are you nursing? I always thought you would be a doctor!"

Margaret and I were given slates (with slate pencil tied to the frame) when very young. The top half had evenly-spaced lines scratched across it. We probably had quite a good grasp of printing before we graduated to exercise books and pencils – the effect of squealing slate pencils on adults was interesting too!

Formal education began with Correspondence School lessons, supervised by Mum. I was in Standard One when we started going to the Waipara School. Margaret and I completed our primary education there and then had correspondence lessons again.

The spare room on the nor'west corner of the house was made into a schoolroom, and we spent a reasonable amount of time there, but the allocation of time to subjects was rather suspect. It didn't take long to do a year's work in the ones we enjoyed. But…!

I majored in English, hygiene, drawing, instrumental drawing and embroidery – We won't say much about French, history and chemistry. I had enjoyed maths at primary school, but we didn't continue with it.

When Harold and our cousin Richard turned five, I started them off by supervising their correspondence lessons.

Richard, Robin, Wallace, Heather Thomson, Betty Page

The next year, the Manahune School started in a room in Dorothy's house, and the teacher lived there too.

Embarrassing Moments

Mum had a knee that would occasionally dislocate and let her down. As a girl she could only mount her bicycle from one side or she would be flat on the ground.

One day, when walking with Dad on the main street of Nelson, her knee suddenly gave way. Dad was horrified and almost cross as he helped her up. He thought people would think that she was drunk.

Harold, as the youngest, was always striving to be equal to his siblings, and was keen to learn from them and emulate their ways.

Mum took him with her to Women's Institute, and he looked a little angel. I can still see Mum cringe as he greeted a kindly Mrs. Hawke with, "I'll chop your head off and squeeze your guts out!"

Farm Implements

A very basic horse drawn implement was the Planet Junior. Pulled by one horse, and guided from behind with two long wood handles, this single furrow plough had about reached the end of its career on Manahune by 1927. Occasionally it was used thereafter to work the vegetable garden.

There were two two-furrow ploughs in use. They worked the same paddock, one behind the other, and a six-horse team drew each. The ploughman either rode on a seat on the back of the plough or walked beside it.

A grubber, a set of discs and a set of tine harrows worked up the ploughed land. A seed drill, followed once more by the harrows, completed the routine for each paddock being worked. Many steps for the plodding horses; and heavy toil for the teamsters driving them and attending to each piece of machinery.

The process, and the flocks of seagulls following the ploughs and pouncing on the worms being turned up in the furrows fascinated us.

Hay was cut by a sickle mower drawn by a single horse, as was the hay rake that dragged it into rows or turned it if necessary.

A reaper and binder cut the barley, wheat or oat crops and bound their stalks into sheaves; three horses in use once again. Carting was done with a spring dray drawn by one horse, or a wagon with three horses, or on the sledge, again with three horses.

A new invention was the hay stacker. It was shaped like a small crane with a forked grab that would be lowered onto the load of hay, and tramped into it. A single horse moved forward to raise the grab, which closed at the same time. The boom was swung round over the stack and the load released. To lower the grab, the horse was backed up.

A horse drawn scoop helped with track maintenance.

Fire

One day we arrived home after school to a distressing sight.

During the day Walter and Dorothy's house had been burnt to the ground and the embers were still smouldering. Dorothy had lit the fire under the copper and gone back to the living room to feed Heather. The next thing she knew, the whole house was in flames. She saved her two babies but lost everything else.

Later that afternoon, Margaret and I were standing under the pine trees on the opposite bank looking across at the burnt out ruins. Suddenly there was a roar above our heads, and a small tip from the pine tree fell at our feet. Our local aviator was making a very close inspection of the scene.

Until their house could be rebuilt Walter's family moved in with us, using the spare bedroom and sitting room and sharing the kitchen.

When the new house was complete, some alterations were made to our house as well. The two verandas were closed in and the kitchen window opening onto the back veranda was removed.

By this time sufficient money had been saved to buy a tractor, but it was all used replacing the house.

Margaret and I had been visiting Quigley's and we were riding our horses home, following a traction engine train. As we rode along the flat above the Mt Donald house, we noticed that the engine had started a small fire on the roadside, and it quickly reached the fence. Margaret galloped her horse up to the engine and signalled to the driver.

45

The gang of men endeavoured to put out the fire and we galloped home to get help.

Margaret went back with Dad and Uncle, and Mum alerted the neighbours by telephone.

The fire was a big one and finished high on the side of Mt Donald. I think a wind change helped control it – that wind change also made things very dangerous for Dad and Margaret.

A traction engine train was coming down the cutting towards our creek. Margaret and I rushed out through the iron-gate to watch. A huge cloud of smoke appeared as the cookhouse chimney caught fire. The engine stopped and the water Joey climbed onto the cookhouse roof with a bucket of water. He poured half of the water down the chimney and the other half over the cook, who just happened to be leaning out of the doorway, looking up.

Fish

Fish was always popular for a Manahune meal. It had been a mainstay for the family meals in Timaru, where Dad and Uncle Walter caught them from the wharf.

Whenever Dad went to Christchurch, he would come home with a parcel of ling, and occasionally with a large crayfish, wrapped in newspaper. The cray was big enough to make a good meal for three adults and three children, and still have some over.

Oysters were a seasonal treat, and I early acquired a liking for them. When we went to the Leithfield beach several times a year we would always dig for pipis, and we all enjoyed them.

Whitebait seemed to be popular with everyone but me. I thought they tasted like eel, which I couldn't abide as a food.

Whenever we went to Christchurch with Dad we always went to Fail's Café in Cashel Street for lunch; usually this was a very large plate of oyster soup with plenty of fresh bread and butter.

One of my early memories is of Uncle Walter sitting on the end of the coal box outside the kitchen. He was threading very large native worms on a piece of thread, which was then made into a ball shape, and attached to some strong cord. He was making a bob to catch eels. The eels' backward pointing teeth would catch in the thread, and they could be flicked out of the creek.

The eels would be skinned to get rid of most of the oil, and the fried in batter. A lot of fine bones meant being very careful when eating.

When we were old enough, dad would take us eeling with a torch at night. There was a reasonable sized pool downstream in Baker's paddock where two creeks joined. The eels would come to the light and endeavour to make a meal of pieces of raw mutton, attached to cod hooks on the end of a piece of cord.

Each of us had one of these lines, and there was plenty of action as eels slithered around on the grass, endeavouring to regain the water. As many as possible were put in a chaff sack to take home.

When Margaret and I were older and allowed to go round the creek on our own, eeling was often on the agenda. We would use a gaff – and on one occasion, this was backed up with a potato fork, when we found a very large eel. It was over four foot long and about ten inches in diameter at the widest point. It was not easy to carry home.

Other fishing at an earlier age included worms on bent pins attached to cotton, which we hopefully dangled in front of cockabullies'. The only bullies we caught were with our cupped hands.

Tadpoles were an easier catch, and if we were quick enough we were able to intercept a frog or two. These were usually reintroduced to the creek after having had a holiday in a bucket or basin up at the house.

There was one special eeling night when Dad took Margaret, Bert, John and me to join the Quigley family, Gordon Baker and a few others. We had made flares by wrapping mutton fat and sacking tightly round the ends of long green poles, and securely wrapping it on with lacing wire. The eeling was done with spears and gaffs. I don't remember if we caught many, but it was a lot of fun.

Food

Although we lived through the slump years we never knew what it was like to be hungry. There was little money, but we had fruit, vegetables, sheep, poultry and eggs, eels, rabbits, milk, cream and butter. The grocer was prepared to barter flour, oatmeal and a little sugar for butter and eggs.

Margaret and I were so young that we had never known any other times, and we were perfectly happy.

Several of the local farmers walked away from their farms, but Dad and Uncle persevered and managed to save enough money to pay their lease. After the slump the Government waived the arrears, but there was much satisfaction in having been able to pay their way.

Breakfast always began with porridge. In summer there would probably be mutton chops, or occasionally eggs. There might also be toast.

Dad liked his main meal midday, and was a meat and at least three vegetables man. He also liked dessert, which mainly consisted of fruit with various accompaniments. On cold days the meal would most likely be preceded by soup.

Tea was usually a bread meal, and often there was cold mutton and salad as well.

In between these main meals were morning and afternoon tea. Morning tea could be scones or homemade buns or, if Mum was having a bread-making spree, there might be a hot bread pinwheel with sugar and cinnamon oozing delectably. Afternoon tea would often feature a slice of Mum's gingerbread or fruitcake, and on special occasions cream sponge.

Hungry Manahune children loved crusts. Babies were given the corner crust from the loaf, and older children helped themselves to a crust whenever they passed the bread bin. It was not uncommon to take a loaf of bread from the bin, and not find one crust on it. Unlike some loaves I have seen since that were only a crust shell, with not a crumb of bread inside!

Throughout the summer raw peas, carrots, turnips, radishes, corn, tomatoes and beans were there for the picking, and an orchard full of fruit filled any vacant corner. It is a wonder that any meals got eaten at all, but they usually did.

There were one or two notable exceptions. Mum thought we would like to try tripe. We didn't.

Occasionally, while Dad was out at rifle shooting, Mum would create a surprise. Sitting on the table next morning would be a small pie dish filled with coconut ice – three layers: white, pink and chocolate. Heaven!

Gardens

At the front of the house the gardens were originally semi-formal.

Gardens either side of the front steps featured climbing roses, jasmine and honeysuckle. A wide curved path led to a little wooden gate; and on each side of this path was a narrow strip of lawn, separating it from a full length bed of assorted roses. Dad had written down all their names in a diary, and knew and loved them all.

Manahune c. 1927 or 1928

A square wooden archway leading to the west lawn had a dark red rose climbing up each side, and intermingling with a honeysuckle that quickly mounded high above the arch. Set into the west lawn was a diamond-shaped bed of roses with a round bed of roses beside it. Near the centre of this lawn was a round flower bed with a dark purple lilac in the middle.

In the centre of the east lawn was a round flowerbed surrounding a white lilac. This lawn was edged on the far side by an *escallonia macrantha* hedge. This had largish stiff dark green leaves with a very spicy smell, and masses of deep reddish-pink flowers. On the other side of the little gate, nor'west shelter was necessary, so a pinus hedge was planted. Inside this was a row of red japonica, which flowered from May to September. Wallflowers and marigolds always self-seeded in this bed.

Margaret

Full length of the west side of the house, geraniums of all colours and varieties flowered continually from late spring till early winter. On the east bloomed violets, columbine, lily of the valley, winter roses and dogtooth violets. Dad had planted a laburnum on that side of the house and rejoiced when its golden cascade of flowers appeared.

Between the house section and the orchard was a fence to deter the chooks, and in front of this a shallow ditch diverted excessive rainwater towards the creek. Between the coal shed and washhouse doors was a small bed of orange-red geraniums.

To the right of the kitchen door was a mandarin tree, and on the left a tallish, orange-red geranium beside a bed of freesias. A rail fence extended from the nor'west corner of the kitchen, and on it grew a very prolific passionfruit next to a single, white-throated red rose that always flowered in September.

A Gros Coleman grape grew in front of Mum and Dad's veranda bedroom.

A pale mauve double lilac grew on the edge of the ditch just past the nor'west corner of the house, and a pink rose rambled over quite a large area along the path to the dairy, encroaching on the area where Walter's tent originally was. A small plant of ivy struggled beside the dairy door and, nearby, clumps of Star of Bethlehem appeared in spring.

In the summer, annuals such as cosmos and cornflowers would fill spaces around the lilac bushes, and violas and alyssum covered the ground beneath the roses.

Over the years the garden evolved, as gardens do. Shrubs were planted, and some of them flourished. A white flowering cherry established well but its pink companion disappeared. Two spirea bushes, a rown tree and a sumac filled in the end of the west lawn; and two hazelnuts flourished by the underground tank. Unfortunately they were both of the same species, so nuts were sparse.

A patch of Russell lupins by the south fence flowered happily for many years. Some of the Escallonia bushes by the little gate expired, and half a dozen new roses were planted in that corner.

The Waipara School ran a garden competition for pupils, and Margaret and I participated. Margaret took over the round bed with the dark coloured lilac, and transformed it – first with annuals, then perennials and bulbs. She maintained it for years, and Margaret's garden always had something special in bloom.

I was allocated a piece of ground in the corner beside where the horses were fed originally. I dug a very odd shape, which more or less fitted in with the area, and opted to plant vegetables. After a few months a long-suffering judge inspected it, and I gained a certificate for participation.

My garden had a rock or two embedded in the soil that I rather liked. I planted a packet of mixed flower seeds and was rewarded with quite a show of colour. Thereafter I would sometimes visit it, and assist nature by delving a bit in the soil, and perhaps removing a spent plant or two. The criterion for a place in that garden was the ability to survive; being vegetable, flower or weed was immaterial.

By the middle of the 1930s, the base of the pine shelterbelt behind the dairy had opened out, and for nor'west protection a pine hedge was planted between the iron-gate and the front of the dairy. A wattle tree opposite the southwest corner of the house thrived, and was set off by yellow doronicum daisies around its base.

The clumps of daffodils in the orchard became so crowded that flowering almost ceased; the divisions from these were planted along the outsides of the rose borders.

Gig

Parked in front of the pine trees, between the dairy and the car shed were the spring cart and the gig,

Until the advent of the wedding present Model T Ford, in 1926, the gig had been Grandma Thomson's only means of transport, to visit her neighbours and attend church. The men had bicycles and horses to ride as other options.

Margaret and I were fascinated with the gig; and especially with its candle-lit-sidelights, necessary when attending evening functions in the district. Although those functions would have been arranged to occur on moonlit nights, one couldn't rely on there being no clouds.

Grasshoppers

"I've got one!" but not for long, as an indignant grasshopper rockets out of the inspection gap between small fingers, probably muttering under his breath, and disappears among the blades of grass several feet away.

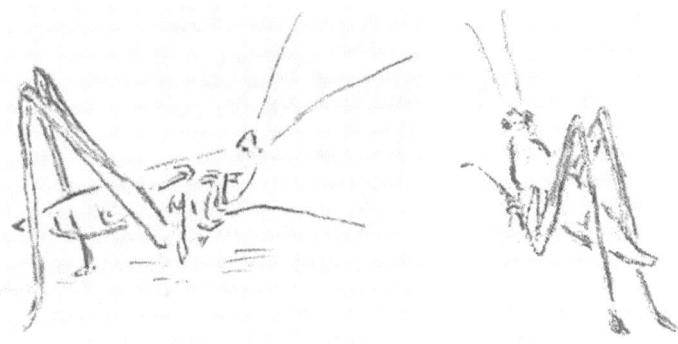

Whenever one walked on the west lawn in summer, there would be an explosion of activity. Black, brown and green grasshoppers leaping waist high to escape these intruders. If one kept very still one could see them clinging to a stalk or balancing on a blade of grass. The slightest movement, and with one mighty bound they were gone.

Harvest

First came the hay. One horse drew the sickle mower. The dried hay was raked into rows with a horse drawn hay rake. Of course it might have to be turned again with the same implement. Two or more rows were raked together. Then there was the manpower bit with large five-tined hayforks.

Margaret on Ginger

The hay was piled onto the sledge with a frame, attached, and transported to the stack site. It was forked from the sledge and formed into a suitable shape. Load after load was carted, until the stack was as high as was convenient for the forkers. Mounded up in the middle, it was then covered with a canvas sheet to keep out the rain. The sheet would have weights hanging from each side. Sometimes the wagon and the spring cart would be used for hay cartage.

Later, a hay sweep reduced the man-hours, and a hay stacker took the burden from the forkers.

The main crop was oats to feed the horses. I can't remember whether they saved their own seed for next year's crop. I do remember the main crop being cut and bound into sheaves by the reaper and binder, drawn by three horses.

The sheaves were picked up, one under each arm, and stood up, leaning against each other. More pairs were added until a self-supporting stook was formed. This could be left in the paddock until it was dry enough to stack.

When we were small, we could only manage one sheaf at a time, but we enjoyed carrying them to where the men would stand them up. Soon we could do the job properly.

Margaret and Alice

When they were ready for stacking, the men would harness three horses to the wagon, and Margaret and I would have the sledge behind three more horses. The sledge had an extension frame added for stacking. We would each have a pitchfork. The bottom layers on the sledge were relatively easy, but had to be properly loaded. Lifting and tossing the sheaves built good arm muscles, as the loads got higher.

Finally, ropes were put across the load, to hold it in place on the slopes. We then climbed on top and drove back to the stack.

Now the sheaves were forked onto the stack, where there were usually two people – one to place the sheaves, and the other to feed more sheaves to the stacker. The rest of us tossed more sheaves up from the sledge and the wagon.

Before long it was necessary to lean a ladder against the stack for the stacker to climb up and down.

The stack was perfectly round and sloped out to the eaves. After that, each row was shorter to form a thatched pointed roof. The butts of the sheaves must also slope slightly downwards to run rainwater off the stack.

A nicely built stack was attractive to look at, as well as being relatively water and wind proof.

It was our ambition to be able to build a stack on our own.

By the time all the sheaves were in, there was a long row of stacks dominating the scene.

Mum would bring our midday meal out to the paddock, and we would already have drinks and snacks with us.

In some years, harvest time would occur in December, and at least one Christmas dinner was eaten in the harvest field; and afterwards we carried right on stacking.

As we worked in the oat field we were not alone on a still day – harvest flies were everywhere. They were about the size of a housefly, and we would flick them off if they landed on our sweaty faces or arms.

When they landed on the frame of the sledge I could study them. Most were finely striped horizontally; black and white, but the backs of others were iridescent blue or green.

The wheat harvest was the same up to the stooking; but the wheat straw was not required for fodder.

A traction engine would arrive in the yard pulling a threshing mill and two whares; one was a cookhouse, and the other sleeping quarters.

There would also be a water cart, a water tank on a horse pulled dray. This was necessary for topping up the boiler.

The whares were left in the yard with the cook, and the traction engine carried on to the wheat field with the threshing mill.

For stook threshing, extra help was required, so the neighbours would appear; usually each driving a spring cart. The mill would be set up in the paddock where the farmer wanted his straw stack; and the carts would already be being loaded with sheaves.

The traction engine was lined up a short distance from the mill, and a five- or six-inch wide laminated canvas, endless belt linked the flywheel on the engine with the driving wheel on the mill. A very skilled operator on the mill would cut the strings and feed the sheaves into the mill. This was very dangerous work.

On one side of the threshing mill was a line of wooden chutes that fed the graded wheat into corn sacks. A group of workers changed the sacks and sewed their tops, and another group would carry and stack the full bags.

A long elevator carried the straw well away from the mill, and two men spread the straw and formed it into a stack. This elevator could be raised, as the stack grew higher.

A large fan inside the mill blew the cavings out of another chute, and they would form a mound too.

The farmers would be very busy carting the wheat sheaves, and there would be a procession of carts to and from the mill.

Meantime back at the cook house, with a large roast sizzling in the oven of the coal range behind him, meditating in the morning sun, the cook sat on the steps. Suddenly, about him materialized a throng of small children, who stayed to chat for a while, before disappearing with a generous slice of sultana cake in hand, as silently (?) as they had come.

Heather, Margaret, Derek, John, Bert, Robin, Alice

The very heavy sacks of wheat were carted on the sledge, and by horse drawn wagon. Some for next year's seed, and the seconds for fowl feed were stored in the wool shed. The remainder was sold.

One year, the stack of sacks of grain caught fire overnight, while still in the paddock. It was presumed that one of the men had dropped a wax match on the pile, and a mouse had chewed it. The whole of the year's wheat harvest was lost.

Over the year, as the store of sacks of chaff dwindled in the woolshed, the traction engine would arrive again, towing a chaff cutter; and sufficient stacks of oats would be cut to refill the shed. The chaff sacks were bigger, but much lighter than the wheat sacks, and we could help with the cartage.

As the last sheaves were forked from the base of an oat stack, the ground would be covered with fleeing mice, chased by enthusiastic children.

Health

John

In general we were pretty healthy. On one of our visits to Nelson, our cousins were diagnosed with whooping cough while we were en route. We were kept apart as far as possible, but all four children caught it. For the three eldest it was unpleasant but bearable, but for John as a three-month-old baby, it was frightening.

When he coughed, Mum had to hold him in an upright position. This meant most of the time. John was left with an umbilical hernia. At about five years of age this was operated on. The post-op instruction included no running, so John developed his own technique; his walk became faster than most people can run.

Tonsillectomy was very common in those days, and after a run of sore throats, Margaret, Bert and I were admitted to Christchurch Hospital to undergo this procedure.

We were in the same room, and settled down reasonably happily for the night, although Bert did receive a smack from a passing nurse, who caught him standing on his head in the hand basin.

Next morning Margaret and Bert were whisked away and operated on. No one bothered about me! When Mum and Dad came to collect us, they were told that I had a cold and couldn't have surgery at present. I still have my tonsils.

At about eight years old I had pneumonia. Sulphonamides had just been discovered, and with their use I made a very good recovery.

During the epidemic of poliomyelitis, my desk mate at school was diagnosed with it, so I was admitted to hospital too. After a few days observation and a lumbar puncture, I was sent home none the worse for wear.

I think we all caught measles and rubella at some stage, and everyone except me had mumps. John caught chicken pox at Boy's High. He came home and passed it on to Margaret and Harold. John made a nice recovery, but Margaret was just coming out in spots on her wedding day. Harold was too ill to go to the wedding.

As a small child I only remember one visit to the dentist. Of course as soon as we entered his waiting room the toothache vanished. I played up too much to be examined and returned home untreated.

Coughs and colds were dealt with by a dose of Lane's Emulsion; and camphorated oil was heated and rubbed on the chest and back. Later, Vicks Vaporub was much in use and Rawleigh's Ready Relief had its place.

When one had a cold we used torn up old sheets for handkerchiefs. These were then burned.

During the whooping cough episode, Mum rubbed cut garlic on our feet. She also tried steam inhalations.

Vaseline was used on chapped lips, and was also rubbed on pitchfork handles to keep them smooth, and blisters on our hands at bay.

Zam Buk was the ointment of choice for grazes and minor irritations. A soak in a weak solution of permanganate of potash dealt with minor skin infections.

Small cuts and infected thorn sites were treated with tincture of iodine -OUCH! -and hydrogen peroxide was poured over larger cuts.

Usually someone could be seen digging out a prickle with a needle. We quickly opted to do our own, and sat on the edge of the back verandah operating on the soles of our feet.

A Saturday dose of 'opening medicine' was the rule in those days, although I'm sure we didn't need it, with all the fruit we ate. Initially it was liquorice powder for children – revolting – and the adults opted for an infusion of senna pods. Fairly early on, Syrup of Figs came on the market and it was bearable. More of my pet hates were daily doses of cod liver oil by the spoonful and, later, malt with cod liver oil.

Barbed wire outriggers were a necessity, to prevent the wire fences being damaged by draught horses with itchy heels.

A single strand of barbed wire near the wool shed caught each of us in turn. When one reached a certain height, the wire became difficult to see when running, and at neck height it was not a pleasant experience.

Bert also tangled with the barbed wire on the fence between the orchard and the track to the cowshed. He rode his bike down the hill too fast to stop at the gate, and his swerve towards the cowshed went too wide!

Most of us had a few falls from horseback, either from a bolting horse – or the horse suddenly shying while trotting.

Harold was unable to bale off the tray of the horse drawn wagon when the horses bolted down hill but he is still alive to tell the tale.

The only broken bones were in Roger's arm when he rolled the Austin; and Dad's ribs when he fell against the frozen edge of a ditch.

John had a lucky escape as a toddler, when the car door opened, and he rolled out onto the road. Mum was extremely relieved to find him sitting on the side of the road crying.

Castor oil needs a space on its own. In a tall, narrow, blue bottle on the pantry shelf, it was gazed upon with horror. As a last resort it was used as a medicine; a layer of orange juice was put in the bottom of a cup, then a spoon full of castor oil, and another layer of orange juice. Encouraging one to drink it was not an easy task!

The second use for castor oil was as a punishment. No orange juice this time!

As four-year-olds, I took my cousin Roger down the hill to see the creek in flood. When we had been collected and returned to the house by very worried parents, out came the blue bottle and a large spoon. More of a deterrent than anything else I could imagine.

The last time I was given castor oil was by my doctor to hurry along my first labour. Thereafter the only use for castor oil in our house was to mix it with ether and use it to run model aircraft motors!

It does have a good use when mixed with zinc as a treatment for bedsores.

Horses

Bess was a wonderful friend to two little girls; she was big and gentle and long-suffering. One could walk underneath her or clamber on her back when she was lying down. If one hung onto her mane and kicked with one's heels, she would carefully regain her feet; and with a bit of persuasion she would walk around the yard. If she stopped by the gate I could climb down, but Margaret could slide down in the open. At a very early age, Margaret learned how to harness Bess into the gig and take us both for a ride round the yard.

Bess had earned her retirement on the farm and had become our playmate.

Among the other horses was Ginger, a much lighter horse than the rest, who was used as a hack.

Dad had a pony he used all the time for sheep work. One day the pony wasn't there and we were told it had died. The previous day we had given it a bucketful of apples. Horses must not be given large quantities of apples! Dad had been very fond of his pony and it was a blow to him.

Walter and Robin on horseback, and Bert standing

There were enough working horses for two six-horse teams and an assortment of foals and young unbroken fillies and geldings.

The stallion was a purebred Clydesdale, as were some of the mares, including Bess. The rest of the horses were half-draught and quarter-draught, and all were named.

Some of the quarter-draughts made good riding horses, and Dad's favourite of these was Nugget. When Dad would walk from the house to the woolshed in the evening to feed the horses, even in the dark, he would feel a horse walking beside him and nuzzling his arm. It would be Nugget, who would stop and Dad would jump onto his back and ride up the hill to the shed.

Initially, the horse feeders were on the outside of the house fence, in the opposite direction to the cowshed. A pile of bags of chaff would sit on the sledge on the house side of the fence. The bags would be covered with a horse cover to keep out the rain.

Horses would be fed morning and evening and, when the supply ran out, three horses would be harnessed to the sledge and a visit made to the woolshed for replacements. Whenever possible we hitched a ride on these occasions.

The harness for the horses lived in the back of the cow shed, where there were pegs on the wall in front of the bails to carry collars and hames, and brackets on the inside of the west wall for saddles. Bridles hung on nails.

There were advantages in feeding the horses nearer to the chaff storage area, although this would entail a twice-daily trek across the creek to the shed.

Upmarket horse feeders were built along the east wall of the wool-shed, and brackets to carry the collars were on the inside of the wall.

Saddles now migrated to brackets on the inside of the garage wall.

Dad did most of the shepherding on the farm while Walter's forte was agriculture. However, they would both work together on whatever job needed to be accomplished, including picking over dags to retrieve a little extra wool, or mending chaff sacks or harness in the woolshed on a wet day.

When we were very tiny Dad would take us with him on his pony; and at quite an early age we graduated to our own mounts. Margaret rode Ginger and I rode Prince, while Dad was on Nugget.

There was much tillage to be done to supply enough oat chaff for about twenty horses, and some wheat for selling and for the fowls. It was also necessary to grow extra green-feed for fattening lambs, and the pastures must be periodically renewed.

First thing in the morning the horses were fed, frequently in the dark, then it was time to milk cows and have breakfast.

The horses were now harnessed and their bridles linked together in threes. The end of a plough line was attached to the bit on the outside of the two side horses. If the plough, or whatever, was already in the paddock, the teamster would ride one of the outer horses of the first three; and have an attached leading rein to the second three.

Alice & Margaret

The sight of two six-horse teams wending their way up the hill was quite spectacular.

Frequently we would go to the shed to help harness the horses, and on their way to work, ride one of the horses as far as the top gate. If possible, we would meet the teams at the top gate in the evening and reverse the process.

In the middle of the day, the working horses would have a meal of chaff in a nose bag hung over their heads, behind the ears.

Margaret and Cephas

When unharnessed at the end of the day, each horse would find a vacant piece of ground, lie down and roll back and forth a few times, before looking round to see if there was anything to eat.

Young horses were broken in on the farm. They had been handled from the time they were born and were well used to people.

When old enough they would have a bridle put on them, and would be tethered for a few hours, and gradually encouraged to accept the bit and the authority of the teamster.

When the time came for them to learn to work, they would be harnessed between two of the steadiest horses, and usually they settled down quite quickly.

Margaret was a very good rider and competed at gymkhanas. She herded cattle and worked the sheep as well as any man, and earned herself an ex-racehorse named Cephos. They worked as a team until Margaret's marriage.

Cephos and Nugget were finally pensioned off and remained on Manahune long after a tractor replaced the horse teams.

Ice Cream

Who doesn't like ice cream?

Once upon a time, like in the early 1930s, ice cream was a very special treat.

It was obtainable in one flavour — vanilla — and was served in cornet cones of two sizes. A smallish orange one held a single scoop, and cost three pence [about two cents] for grownups; and a penny one, that was tiny, and pink, and held about a third of a scoop. Of course this was for children — they wouldn't be able to manage any more of this cold stuff!

At first only some of the grocers' shops stocked ice cream, and then only in the summer. After all, who would want ice cream in the winter? Who? Inhabitants of Manahune of course!

It's snowing! Is it going to settle? Will there be enough?

About three times during my first ten years, there was enough ! And we made ice cream!

When enough snow had settled, a mixture of thin custard with plenty of whipped cream stirred in was put in shallow containers, securely covered for protection from enquiring cats, and very carefully placed at the back of the house behind the tank stand. Next morning it was inspected and carefully stirred. It had to be eaten before any thaw set in.

Very occasionally Dad would come home with a whole pint of ice cream. This was immediately divided out into saucers, and a spoonful of homemade raspberry jam decorated the top of each.

We all had our preferences as to how we ate it, whether fast, or a slow savouring. Bert had his own technique – his saucer was placed on top of the coal range. When that icecream had lost its chill, and was sufficiently runny, Bert would enjoy his share.

Sometime after electricity was installed in 1938, we owned a refrigerator, and ice cream lost some of its magic – but not too much!

Incidentals

Just before Bert was promoted from cot to bed, Mum left her veranda bedroom for a few minutes, leaving a lighted candle on the shelf above the bed. A loud bang made her hurry back, and she found a rather confused little boy sitting in the middle of her bed.

Apparently he had climbed out of his cot and onto the double bed, where he found a round of .22 ammunition that had fallen from Dad's pocket. Hi picked it up and held it in the candle flame.

How did Roger break the sitting room window?
He stood between a cousin and the window.
The aim was good and the throw was better.
The gumboot's flight was straight and true
But Roger ducked.

Dad transports eggs from fowl house to pantry in his hat.
The eggs are fresh and the hat is full.
A cricket ball descends from the sky.
It is now in the hat with the eggs.
Dad isn't pleased.

John and Joey

Joey

Joey was part of the family. He knew us all by name and could call us individually, using Mum's voice. Visitors were not particularly welcome; and had to watch their step, and their ankles.

Joey had a favourite, Harold.

For a few years from about 1945 they were inseparable. Harold's bed was on the front veranda; and in the morning when Mum went to call Harold, she would find two heads on the pillow; one of them was black-and-white and sported a beak and two beady eyes. Joey was a magpie.

Joey was free and could come and go as he pleased. One day he just didn't return, and we never did discover his fate.

Kitchen

The centre of life at Manahune was the kitchen.

It was long and narrow (9ft by 17ft), warm and bright, and filled with companionship, laughter, music and delicious cooking smells. It was very crowded, and only now do I appreciate Mum's cheerful patience, as she cooked tasty meals for all of us; and manoeuvred hot saucepans and baking dishes to and from the coal range without anyone being burnt.

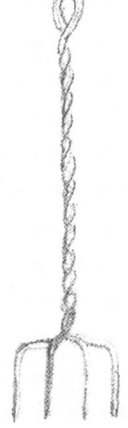

The coal range was in the centre of the north end. It had SCOTT embossed on its oven door, and the firebox could be opened out, to give the effect of an open fire – wonderful for toasting thick slices of bread impaled on homemade wire toasting forks.

A large heavy kettle always simmered on the stovetop, and was often accompanied by a stockpot boiling mutton bones and vegetables for soup.

I can just remember Grandma Thomson sitting in a wicker chair to the right of the stove; up until then, the kitchen would have been her domain. When Mum and Dad first married, the whare was so tiny that Grandma only allowed Mum to help with the vegetables, preserving and the dishes.

Mum's private area was their tent, and she spent the first eight months of marriage out on the farm with Dad – a wonderful honeymoon.

By the end of those eight months the Manahune house was completed and Mum and Grandma divided the work of home and garden, not to mention cows, between them.

Grandma was a wonderful cook. After years of penury in her middle age, as she struggled to earn enough to feed herself and her growing sons, this was a time of relative comfort and wealth. She delighted in producing three cooked meals a day, as well as lavish morning and afternoon teas, for her family and for whosoever.

In the middle of each long side of the kitchen was a door. That on the east opened into the scullery, and the west lead-lighted door opened to the outside. On either side of this door was a transomed, casement window with six small panes, set off with white muslin curtains with tiny embossed green dots.

At the house end, a door close to the outside wall opened into the hallway. In the southeast corner, a corner cupboard had doors below a full-sized shelf. Above that, a series of narrow shelves extended along each wall. The cupboard contained mending equipment and correspondence, and the dictionary.

In the northwest corner was the cylinder cupboard beside the coal range. There was also a tap in this corner, where one could get hot water without wasting the cold water in the pipe to the scullery. The cylinder could boil madly and spout hot water on to the roof.

In front of the coal range was a sturdy fireguard that hooked into a staple on each side. On this guard would hang an oven cloth, and frequently baby washing, or other garments that needed a final airing.

Above the range was a rack, handy for heating plates or placing the odd pot lid. On a hook, inside the guard, hung poker and toasting forks.

Along the scullery wall was a form with loose cushions on it, behind a long narrow table. A row of chairs tucked under the front of the table.

To the left of the outside door was the wireless, powered by two car batteries that sat on a shelf below. The main set was fairly big and cumbersome. With it some exciting moments were celebrated – such as the arrival of Kingsford Smith in New Zealand after crossing the Tasman in his plane, *the Southern Cross*. We also followed the adventures of "Marco Polo" and "Westward Ho". During wartime, Big Ben heralded the 9 o'clock news from London.

To the south of the scullery door was a long sofa, until it was ousted by the piano and then took up residence against the opposite wall.

A wicker chair sat against the end wall. The floor was covered by printed linoleum and a few mats.

In 1938 an electric stove was installed to the north of the outside door.

There was always a container of flowers on the table, anything from a handful of wild flowers, or violets, to an arrangement of roses or lilac; and once a year Dad would always stop on the way home from Waipara, to allow us to pick a big bunch of the first wattle from the roadside.

The kitchen was always well lit. in the centre of the ceiling was a petrol-lamp with a mantle. It produced a light that was equal to the electric light that replaced it. There were two other petrol lights, in the sitting room and in the hallway. The petrol was in a pressurized tank complete with pressure gauge and foot pump, and kept in a cupboard on the back veranda.

On the wall near the hall door hung the telephone. A wooden compartment contained two batteries. The receiver hung on a hook on the left and there was a handle on the right that one turned to make it ring. The signals were Morse code, with one turn of the handle for short and three for long. At mouth-height was a microphone that one spoke into, with two bells above it.

We were on a party line with six other families that we could ring directly; or by making one long ring we could reach the telephone exchange operator, who would connect one to any other number – within calling hours.

If one wished to use the phone one would lift the receiver and say, "working". If there was no response, one could go ahead. After a call was finished, a short ring was made to show the line was clear.

The Waipara telephone exchange was in one of the houses east of the hotel.

By our teen years, a small electric-powered radio sat on the corner cupboard; the table was against the veranda wall, and the sofa had taken the table's place against the scullery wall.

The remainder of the whare consisted of the scullery, the pantry and Grandma's tiny bedroom.

After a disagreement with Grandma, the builder had placed the built-in tank stand directly outside Grandma's bedroom window, about four feet from the house.

The pantry was in the middle and occupied about two thirds of the depth of this area – Grandma's room and the scullery were full length.

On the outside of the pantry wall was a meat safe This had two slatted shelves and was covered on three sides with fine wire gauze. A door opened into it at the back of a bench in the pantry, and it could be accessed through doors on the outside as well.

Beneath the bench under the meat safe was a locked cupboard that contained caustic soda, and any other dangerous substances.

The bench continued round the left side, and under it were bins for bread, flour and sugar. Above that bench and all the right side of the pantry, there were shelves from floor to ceiling.

On the floor stood unopened bags of sugar and flour, a four-gallon tin of honey and a large crock that was frequently full of blackcurrant jam. There came the day when the pantry door was left open and a crawling Harold discovered the crock. At arm's length, Mum held up a baby covered with blackcurrant jam from head to foot.

Crockery and cutlery all had their place in the pantry.

The scullery had a door opening outside on the northwest corner. A solid wooden bench with a sink set into it occupied the north wall.

Above it was a board with a row of nails driven into it, on which hung cooking utensils, and beneath it a shelf for pots and pans. Along the back of the pantry wall was a full-length towel rail.

On the east wall was a six-paned, fixed sash window. I loved that window. In the winter ice ferns would appear. They grew from the lower corner, and some days they would cover the whole of the window. They were beautiful, but perhaps they made a statement about the temperature in the scullery.

Lawns

Surrounding the house were quite extensive lawns; not the sort of lawns one could reasonably expect to see when admiring any picture-perfect, prize winning garden, but down-to-earth, daisy - and dandelion – friendly, come-and-play-on-me lawns.

They had to be kept well mown; not from choice, but of necessity. A push mower rebels if the grass gets too long, and its pusher rebels even more.

As is still the case today, children show the most interest in mowing lawns when the task is almost beyond them. I remember the pride in a few yards mown, and the achievement of mowing a complete lawn.

Dad maintained the push mower himself, keeping the cutting blades sharp, and the working parts well oiled and adjusted.

Other grass cutting implements were the sickle and the scythe.

The sickle was a curved blade with a wooden handle. One would hold the heads of grain or whatever, in one hand and sever their lower stalks with the sickle. There were two in the shed, but I never saw them put to serious use.

The scythe was a different matter. A long, tapered and slightly curved cutting blade was attached to a long, specially shaped, vertical wooden shaft, with two short handles on it. It had been the method of reaping crops and hay before mechanical reapers were invented.

Mum was an expert with the scythe. She could scythe cut the orchard grass in short order. A sharpening stone carried in her apron pocket kept that blade razor sharp.

We were not allowed anywhere near when the scythe was being used.

Later of course, the push mower was pensioned off, and its work taken over by a motor driven model.

Originally there was a small patch of daisies growing in the lawn near the tank stands. Over the years several more patches appeared. When Dad mowed the lawn, he would carefully mow round those patches of daisies, without beheading any.

Letter Writing

On one of the narrow shelves above the corner cupboard sat bottles of ink and dip pens, also a fountain pen, with its own reservoir of ink. These would be used daily. Dad had farm records to keep; and he was a good letter writer.

There were elderly aunts in London, and a cousin in Canada, who received long newsy letters from their New Zealand nephew and cousin.

Later, when Mum's Uncle George retired and went to Nelson, Dad would write to him every week. Uncle George looked forward to those letters.

Mum did a little letter writing too, and Margaret was the main letter writer in our generation.

The bottles of blue, green and red ink had other uses too. Have you ever sat the cut end of a daffodil or snowflake stalk in a bottle of ink overnight?

Long Drop

Through the tall, fowl netting-covered gate, beside the garage, strategically facing the morning sun, was the long drop.

With the lean-to-roof, corrugated iron cladding, wooden seat with cut out hole, and a No.8 wire hook-and-staple fastener, it was quite up-market, compared with some I have known.

The long drop was very necessary during the summer, when the water supply was limited. It could also be an advantage when the house was full of family, and over-nighting guests.

Walter prided himself on never using the inside flush toilet.

One did not put anything into the long drop that one wished to see again. Occasionally it was the recipient of broken glass; and at least once, a torch. The torch lit up its humble surrounds for an hour or two, and then quietly succumbed.

Cleaning the long drop was not high on my list of favourite pursuits. Sweep down spider webs and any protesting spiders. Sweep out pine needles. Scrub seat and floor with sand soap and bucket of hot water with a dash of Jeys fluid. Replenish supply of newspaper squares impaled on No.8 wire. If left to their own devices in the open-topped box, a nor'west wind and open door would soon spread them throughout the orchard.

The final luxury was a copy of the Auckland Weekly – mainly for reading purposes, on account of its particularly high gloss!

Memories

One of my earliest memories is of Margaret and me in the pram, large and with fairly big wheels, and Mum pushing us up the hill to the little iron gate at the low corner of the lawn.

I have vague memories of us coming along the road from Quigley's too.

The most vivid part of the memory is of the pram sticking in the gateway, and Dad coming to help free it.

It would have been a tiring afternoon for Mum, with the hills and shingle road – the hills much steeper than now – and three creeks to ford. I don't know whether she took off her shoes, or just waded through.

Another intended visiting afternoon, probably two or three years later as Bert was the baby, Mum got Margaret and me ready first; brushed hair and nice ribbons, and our only good frocks – this was early thirties in the middle of the slump. She then attended to herself and Bert.

Margaret and I wandered through the orchard, and the lovely clay slide on the gully bank opposite called to us. We had a marvellous time. When Mum found us she wasn't pleased. That visit didn't eventuate.

There, under the pine trees not too far from the long drop, was a pile of old paint tins. They had to be investigated. What was this black stuff? It was a little bit runny. It could be stirred with pine twigs.

It stuck to pine twigs and our fingers. What about faces? Yes!

Once again Mum was not pleased. As yet she hadn't learned that tar could easily be removed with butter. Scrubbing brush and soap left skin very red and sore.

I was milking a cow, probably automatically, as I leaned my head on her flank and gazed out to the cow yard. It began to snow without any wind. The flakes drifted down and I began to float – an amazing sensation.

Whenever I see snow falling, I remember, and hope for a repeat of that moment, but the conditions since then, have never been quite the same.

In my early teens I decided to weed one of the long rose beds. No one had done anything in the flower gardens for a long time, and in the dry conditions the ground was rock hard.

At lunchtime it was mentioned that I had done some weeding, and Dad immediately said he would dig the ground over before he went back to work. I told him that there wasn't much ready, but he said that didn't matter. His face was a picture as, spade in hand, he surveyed two square feet of bare ground.

I loved lying on my stomach, looking over the back of the sledge, while listening to the squeal of the iron shod runners, and smelling the burnt rock as they struck sparks from the greywacke rocks, embedded in the track.

Mum and Dad would often hold hands under the table at lunchtime. Then after lunch they would wander round the garden looking at the roses, still holding hands.

Lila and Bert

Mushrooms

Mushrooms were enjoyed by everyone. Most years they were quite plentiful and we soon learned the best places to go for the various varieties.

Horse mushrooms grew on the woolshed flat, and were plentiful on the trig hill.

Field mushrooms flourished where the ground was left undisturbed; particularly around the gullies and any pastures several years old.

I located a patch of medium sized brown-topped ones with good pink gills. They grew among the rocks on the homestead hill, and every few days in mushroom season, I would run there and back to make sure I didn't miss any.

Music

Mum and Dad were both musical. Dad had had one piano lesson as a child. The teacher had a packet of fish and chips on the end of the keyboard, and ate them as she taught. When she put her greasy fingers on Dad's hand, that was too much, and from then on he was self-taught. He also played the violin and the accordion, playing for dances in the early days at Waipara.

Walter had a violin too, but I don't remember hearing him play.

Dad sang a lot as he went about his work; sea shanties, and music hall favourites from the beginning of the century; also Gilbert and Sullivan excerpts. Grandma Thomson sang a lot.

Mum had had piano lessons for quite a few years, and she played nicely. She had a pile of good piano music, and she enjoyed singing. Her father sang well, and her sister Hilda was a natural piano player.

Our earliest instrumental music was enthusiastic, if lacking other qualities. Small cheap mouth organs, the odd tin whistle, a blade of grass stretched between the thumbs, and of course the hair comb with a piece of tissue paper. We loved to play with Dad's accordion on the odd, very special occasion.

Margaret was a very good singer and could sing harmony. We would sing together as we milked the cows, and this was fine in general. However, if Margaret wished to raise the tone of the recital with some harmony, my deficiencies appeared. I always sing along happily with the loudest voice.

While we were attending the Waipara School, Mum and Dad went to Christchurch one day and came home with a piano. Mum and Dad both enjoyed playing it for a little time in the evenings, and we experimented. Margaret was very good at *Chopsticks*. I didn't have much to offer.

When we were at home doing our correspondence course, it was easier to fit in music lessons. Dad took us to Christchurch on the train, and we found the studio of a Miss A. Gibb. She heard us play a little, decided where we were at, and agreed to teach us.

We also had one or two ballroom dancing lessons over those weeks. We started travelling to town each week by train.

Before long, Miss Gibb agreed to come by train to Waipara each week, if enough pupils could be found to fill the day between trains. We collected her from the train and gave her dinner, and extra pupils came to Manahune to be taught.

The piano had originally been in the kitchen, but now it was necessary to have it in the front room, where a fire was lit on cooler days. It made a very satisfactory studio for Miss Gibb. As I remember, she was teaching there up to the time I started nursing.

Neighbours

The families living on the Lake Road extension of the Glenmark Drive had much in common, and periodically visited each other.

Mr and Mrs Eddy Blake owned and farmed Glenlake. They were followed by the Coe family and then the Slosses.

Colin and Winnie Mowart farmed to the west of the road and the Barnes Estate was on the east, adjacent to Manahune. Mr Barnes had had a stroke, and was lovingly cared for by his widowed daughter, Mary Aydon, and her son, Alf. Mrs Barnes and Mr Aydon had both succumbed in the 1918 influenza epidemic. Margaret and I would visit Auntie Mary with Joan Quigley, whose mother Amy had been a Barnes. Norman Mahon took over this property.

Between the Mowart property and Mt Donald, was the McMillan farm, which extended through to the Waikari valley; the farmhouse was on the Waikari side.

Murray McMillan would always call at Manahune for a meal, when he came on horseback to attend to the sheep at the back of their farm. He was also able to use the Manahune wool shed as required.

Brian and Agatha WynWilliams farmed Mt Donald. Their three children were quite young at that stage.

Next there was the domain of 'Uncle Frank' and 'Auntie Amy' Quigley and their two children, Joan and Derek. Joan and Derek were contemporaries of Margaret and Bert respectively.

Shellrock extended behind Glenbrae and was farmed by Bert and Zeta Herbert and their two boys.

The farm south of the Shellrock Drive was farmed first by the O'Carroll family, and then by the Allison family.

Glenalton was the home of Alton and Maud Uren and their children Steve, Dorothy, Leila and Mervyn.

Tommy and Mrs Baker and son Gordon owned the property between Manahune and the Glenmark Homestead.

South of the Homestead, on the opposite side of King's Rd, Mr and Mrs McGuckin had their farm. Daughter Phyllis lived with her parents, and Len and Thelma with son David, lived in a nearby cottage.

Who is my neighbour? Each one of those wonderful compassionate folk, who banded together to complete the tillage, and the drilling of that large steep paddock where Walter had his accident. This gave Dad time to get over some of the trauma of that day, before having to work that paddock again.

Harold, Bert, Bert jnr, John, Alice, Margaret, Heather, Robin, Walter, Richard

Dad was devastated by the loss of his only sibling. The only time they hadn't worked together was for about two years in their mid-teens, when they worked on two different types of farm; Walter learning agriculture, and Dad, mixed farming.

Dad had not only lost his brother, but he was now solely responsible for the running of the farm, and for the welfare of two households, including nine children. In the course of the first few weeks Dad's hair turned completely white.

Margaret did the work of a man, as she assisted Dad in those years, and Bert also was working on the farm at a level beyond his age.

New Life and Death

Mum's first pregnancy finished as a miscarriage, while she and Dad were still living in the tent at the bottom of the orchard. The doctor was called, but he was too drunk to assist. Mum's sister Hilda looked after her.

Margaret and I followed at fifteen-month intervals. We were both born at St Helen's Hospital, where Mum had trained in Christchurch.

Margaret Sansom brought Mum and me home in her car. In the last creek on the road before Manahune, the car became stuck due to

Margaret, Dorothy, Walter, Roland

flooding and had to be pulled out by Dad with a horse.

In 1931 while Mum was expecting Bert, Grandma Thomson, aged 64, became ill and died within a week. She had not been very well for some time but had refused to see a doctor. An unfortunate decision since the diagnosis was diabetes, and she could have been treated, if she had been seen sooner.

Bert arrived at shearing time. He was born at home, and there was a live-in-midwife. Dad and Uncle slept in the wool shed until she left.

John also was a home birth. Margaret and I were now having correspondence lessons, and it was decided to have someone to live in to mind the three older children and look after things until Mum was back on her feet again.

A live-in midwife was also present.

The home help was Dorothy Cookson. Walter and Dorothy became engaged, a house was built for them near the road and within three months they were married.

Walter Robin arrived the next year, and Heather Estelle the year after. Richard Kenneth was born in 1938, the same year as Harold.

Emma Florence Fendall

I think all of Dorothy's children were born at Rangiora, as was Harold.

Grannie Fendall came down from Nelson to look after our family when Harold was born and stayed for several months. She returned to Nelson for a few months, then came back and spent most of her last two years at Manahune. She died in 1940, aged 79.

In 1944, aged 49, Walter was killed when he fell and hit his head on the plough, while ploughing a hill side on Manahune. This happened on Mum's birthday. For this birthday, I had secretly made Mum a sponge cake, and I was decorating it in the schoolroom when Dad came home distraught. Later that day Mum found the forgotten cake and came and thanked me for it. It was many years before Mum was able to enjoy her birthday again.

Six weeks later, on my birthday, Dorothy gave birth to Wallace Donald.

Marriages

Jan 20 1926
> Albert Archibald Thomson – Lila Cobourg Fendall
> St Paul's Glenmark The Rev. F. P. Fendall

Oct. 1934
> Walter Richard Thomson – Dorothy Evelyn Cookson
> St Peter's, Upper Riccarton Archdeacon George York and
> the Rev. Herbert York

Births

| May | 1927 | Lila Margaret | St Helen's, Christchurch |
| Aug | 1928 | Alice Florence | St Helen's, Christchurch |

Nov	1931	Albert Federick Walter	Manahune
July	1934	John David	Manahune
Sept	1935	Walter Robin	
Jan	1937	Heather Estelle	
Oct	1938	Harold Stanley	Rangiora
	1938	Richard Kenneth	
Aug	1944	Wallace Donald	

Deaths

June 19	1931	Alice Louise Thomson	Manahune
Nov 16	1941	Emma Florence...Fendall	Manahune
July 8	1944	Walter Richard Thomson	Manahune

Nightmare

This nightmare recurred two or three times.

Margaret and I were on the back seat of the Model T Ford. The canvas top was up but it seemed very flimsy to me. The car stopped in the middle of the ford, in the creek below the house, and was approached by large cows with huge horns.

I never thought to tell Mum about this; but wonder now if it actually happened when I was tiny, since cows are so inquisitive.

Except for the house cows, I was always nervous among cattle.

Alive, Bert, Magaret

Orchard

When Dad and Uncle Walter were lads growing up in Timaru, money was in very short supply. Their mother cleaned offices to support them, and they worked after school, and caught fish from the wharf to help keep food on the table.

One of Dad's few pet hates was stewed apple with plain boiled rice. I suspect it had been their staple diet at one period.

When the two boys established Manahune, one of their dreams was to have a Garden of Eden-like orchard. By the time Mum and Dad married, that orchard had begun to flourish.

The whole of the Manahune house flat was ringed with three rows of pine trees; and the slopes above and below were covered with a plantation of these trees. Dad and Uncle had collected pine cones while working at the Homestead and had saved and grown the seeds. These were carefully nurtured, and the men would carry buckets of water up from the creek to see them through their first summer.

At the base of the hill at the top of the flat, they planted a row of poplars. Hares ring-barked and killed all but one of these. At the base of the plantation above the creek they planted a seedling blue gum tree, also from the Homestead.

By this time they had moved from the tent site by the creek, up to the house flat. Grandma had moved up from Timaru and was sleeping in the whare. Dad also had a room in the whare and Uncle slept in his tent.

By now the property had its boundary fence complete and was steadily being divided into smaller paddocks. The woolshed had been built. With some shelter and a little more time and money, it was time to think about the orchard. The northwest corner of the flat was cultivated, and young trees and berry fruit bushes obtained.

The row nearest the whare consisted of red and black currants on the east, and about six quince trees from opposite the whare to the west. Behind the quinces were five Cox's Orange apple trees and another quince. Vegetables grew behind the currants.

The third row had two or three Winter Cole pears to the east and continued with assorted apples, mainly Sturmers.

Row four began with about four William's Bon Cretian pears and continued with a mixture of other pears and apples. Row five was mainly apples, beginning and ending with different varieties of cooking apples, and included two Worcester Pearmains.

Row six started with a peach, and continued with two very early apples, before changing to assorted plums, and finishing with a nectarine.

Row seven had an apricot, some nectarines, and continued with more varieties of plums.

Starling

The rest of the rows were shorter as they followed the curve of the gully. There were about three more rows that included two very late pears, two walnuts, a damson plum, early peaches, three cherries, a few apples and about seven assorted apricots.

In the final row, between the cherries and a tall apricot, was a row of different varieties of gooseberry; red, yellow, green, hairy and smooth. There were also some white currants.

In between the rows of young fruit trees were planted rows of raspberries, and a place was found for loganberries and boysenberries. A thornless blackberry struggled to survive against the back wall of the whare, and a mandarin thrived by its front door.

The first grapevine on Manahune succumbed to the effects of an over generous supply of surplus skim milk.

In all there were about one hundred fruit trees planted initially, as well as the berries. To complete the effect, seven or eight varieties of daffodil and some snowflakes were planted along the rows of apples, and a row of violets bordered the full west end of the orchard.

The only disappointment was the quinces. They were supposed to supply a visual feast of blossom and fruit, but were apparently sterile. However, the lone quince behind them endeavoured to make up for their deficiencies and supplied us with all the fruit we needed.

The raspberries had disappeared before I was old enough to appreciate fruit, but Mum said she had spent many long hours picking them for sale. The canes had been rather short, and she had found it hard on her back.

Surplus fruit was often given away, but I think some may have been sold, as well as the raspberries.

We never knew life without an abundance of fruit and knew the varieties of each. In summer our midday meal was often a picnic in the orchard, under the peach and apricot trees. Dessert was pick-your-own.

Plums, peaches, nectarines, pears, gooseberries and especially apricots were bottled. Bucketsful would be picked during the day, and we would all sit round and prepare and pack them during the evening. Mum would top up the jars with syrup and put the rubber rings and glass tops in place. They were then cooked in a water bath in the copper.

The defunct grapevine was replaced with a Gros Coleman grape, planted beside the back veranda. This grape thrived, and was trained over a pergola above the adjacent path. Much of the fruit was against the edge of the veranda roof, making it easily accessed by enterprising children. One could ascend beside the meat safe, cross the lean-to-roof over the pantry and kitchen, and descend the eighteen-inch drop to the lean-to veranda roof.

At times the line-up of grape-eating children on the roof consisted of Joan and Derek Quigley, Margaret, Alice, Bert, John, Robin and Heather Thomson.

At least Mum knew where we were, and we could hand bunches down to her, (and Richard and Harold).

The Gros Coleman vine finally got mildew and was replaced by a Black Hamburg, trained over the same framework, but planted on the opposite side of the path.

Pipes

Walter and Cousin Roland both smoked pipes. They would have a tobacco pouch of cut tobacco in their pocket, and when they wanted to smoke, would turn the pipe upside down and tap out the spent ash.

The pipe might need reaming out with a pocket knife at this stage.

Cut tobacco leaf was piled into the bowl of the pipe and tamped in with a tobacco stained forefinger. The top of the tobacco was lit with a match while the smoker sucked air through the pipe to create a draught. They would then puff away contentedly.

When I was fairly young, I was sitting in the sun on the edge of the veranda eating a piece of cake. I noticed Roland's tobacco pouch lying on the veranda nearby. Who could resist playing with the zip and looking after the pouch until reclaimed?

When Roland opened the pouch, and found the cake crumbs mixed through his tobacco, I received a good sharp slap on the bare leg. The only time Roland ever raised his hand, I think, to any of us.

Plough Lines

Plough lines were ropes that were used to steer the horse teams, when ploughing or drawing other implements.

They needed to be quite long, as they were fastened to the bit on an outside lead horse, then through a ring on the harness of the horse directly behind. The other end did the same on the other side, with enough length in the middle to reach easily to the ploughman, as he sat on the seat of the plough behind.

The rear trio of horses needed a shorter line, which was held with the first one – two lines in each hand of an alert ploughman. Sometimes he would walk beside the plough, and needed to have sufficient length to guide the horses safely without getting tangled with the machinery.

The plough lines had a reasonable life span, but had to be strong enough to control the horses in an emergency.

Dad made new plough lines on a regular basis, and we loved to help him. He had adapted a brace for this job; a long nail bent into a hook was firmly held in the chuck, and a weight on a loop of binder twine was attached to the centre of the brace.

On the gatepost was a wire hook, and on the far corner of the coalhouse was a strong nail half driven in, and with its head cut off.

The end of a new ball of binder twine was tied in a loop, and slipped over the hook on the brace, while Dad stood opposite the near end of the coal bin. We would take it in turns to carry the centre of a loop of twine down to the gate and slip it over the hook. There were now four lengths of twine, and the end was cut and attached to the brace.

With the head of the brace between his hands, Dad would swing the weight clockwise until the cord had shortened enough to slip from the hook on the brace, to the nail on the wall. This was repeated twice. The last time, the two cords were slipped off the nail and joined the third, which was already on the hook.

Now the weight was swung anti-clockwise to ply the rope, which was stretched as it was spun.

The end of the new rope was slipped off the hook, and an over-hand knot tied at the end. Dad would stretch it again, and let it go a few times to release any over-spin. We would run down to the gate, slip the far end off the wire, and bring it back to Dad. He tied another knot and loosely coiled the rope.

The final step was to singe off the loose fibres over a burning newspaper out in the yard.

Sometimes the ends of the new plough line were spliced, but usually the knot sufficed.

Quotes

From Dad:

A man convinced against his will is of the same opinion still!

Faint heart never won fair lady.

This won't buy the baby a bath.

I didn't come down in the last shower!

From a thank-you letter.

E— was going to be very greedy with the chocolates, but me stopped her, me did.

Questions

On the heights of Manahune are two types of rock. On the south boundary is an outcrop of sedimentary rock filled with sea-shells. At what stage was sea level at this height? Or was the outcrop raised by a seismic event?

On the tops and slopes of the highest hills is volcanic rock. This is in large sheets beneath the topsoil. Was lake Raupo the crater of an extinct volcano?

For many years moa bones were washed down the creek by every flood. When did the last moa roam Manahune's hills and valleys?

Relatives ~ Cousins

Isla, Campbell, Marie, Murray, Lorna

Mum's father and mother were both members of large families.

Mum's only cousins on the York side of the family were the children of Dudley and Hedley Irvine of Takaka. They were Isla, Campbell, Lorna, Murray and Marie.

Marie was a trained nurse, and came to Manahune to nurse Grannie Fendall, in her final Week of life. She took Margaret and me back to Takaka with her for a week's holiday. We stayed with Lorna and Dennis Hope and their two oldest children, on their dairy farm, and met the rest of the Takaka relations. We then visited the Kings in Richmond, and the York aunts and uncles in Stoke.

The Fendall family produced many more cousins.

One day Mum had a phone call from her cousin Roland Austin Fendall. He had been raised in the North Island and had been transferred to the Kaiapoi branch of the BNZ. Could he visit?

An unknown cousin from the North Island visiting simple farming folk? We would do our best!

Snowy linen appeared on the extension table in the sitting room, with matching serviettes, gleaming silver and polished glass; flowers everywhere, and a repast that Royalty would have appreciated. Even children on their best behaviour!

Roland tucked in and appeared to enjoy it all.

Finally he moved his chair back slightly from the table, leaned back, and made the proclamation that forevermore promoted him from sitting room to kitchen, as a fully-fledged family member.

"My guts are rotten."

Cousin Roland came to spend every second weekend at Manahune, for all the years he was at Kaiapoi. From Lawrence he was more restricted to long weekends, and from Kaitaia he still managed more than one visit a year. On his return to the South Island, his visits to his second home became more frequent again, until, while he was working in Nelson, he met and married Jess Lessels. Roland was very patient with children, and wherever he went on his long walks over Manahune, there was a Pied Piper-like trail behind him. Frequently he would have his .303 or .22 with him, and he taught the older children how to shoot rabbits.

A windup gramophone and boxes of records travelled in Roland's car, and we were treated to a wide range of music.

Games of 500 round the kitchen table in the evening, sometimes with outrageous cheating, and rough-and-tumbles with the boys, were part and parcel of those weekends.

Roland never arrived empty-handed, and there

Roland Fendall

would be bags of bananas and other goodies, to help with the meals.

On one particularly memorable weekend, a game in the hall had reached a climax of rowdiness, and Mum attempted to quieten things down. She opened the door from the kitchen and let forth a very un-Mum-like tirade. There on his own stood a sheepish Roland; everyone else had vanished.

Even before Roland's visits began, there were Auntie Margaret and Uncle Harold. Margaret Sansom was Mum's best friend at school in Rangiora, and this was a lifelong friendship.

Auntie Margaret and Uncle Harold were engaged. She was the Infant Mistress at a Christchurch primary school, and Harold Southerill owned a little grocery shop on the corner of Salisbury and Madras Streets, and lived above it.

Margaret Southerill

They would stay for the weekend and sometimes Auntie Margaret would stay longer during school holidays. Uncle H. enjoyed playing Euchre, and this would fill the evenings, except when Roland was there too – when it became a toss-up between euchre and 500.

Auntie Margaret knitted almost continuously. Seemingly it was automatic, as she never seemed to have to look at it. She could talk continuously too.

In the May school holidays 1945, Aunty Margaret and Uncle Harold took Margaret and me for a holiday at the Franz Josef Glacier Hotel. We travelled in their Citroen car to Springfield, from whence, with car on a wagon and us in a carriage, we boarded the train. We continued by car from Otira. The weather was beautiful and we had a wonderful time, including a flight over the glaciers.

Harold Southerill, Margaret, Alice, Margaret Sansom

Later the same year, Auntie Margaret and Uncle Harold arrived at Manahune with Auntie Margaret wearing a Wedding Ring – the end of a seventeen-year engagement.

They moved into a cottage on Hoon Hay Road and created a lovely garden there.

Mum's cousins, Eileen Hamilton and Norman Fisher, married and lived on a farm at Bennets, near Oxford. They adopted a little girl, Anne. For many years they visited Manahune on the Sunday of Labour Weekend.

Eileen's brother Leonard Hamilton and his wife Molly had three children; Irene, Brian and Audrey.

Audrey was a year or two older than Margaret, and when she was twelve she came to Manahune for a school holiday.

Audrey

Thereafter she spent as many holidays as possible with us. She played the piano well, and was good fun.

Brian first visited us when he was in the Fleet Air Arm before embarking for Canada. He played the piano beautifully and was a Cathedral Chorister. Sadly, he did not return from the war.

We did not meet Irene until later. Her fiancé was killed in the war, and a very sad Irene came to stay. She fitted in well and enjoyed being with the Southerills and our family, and soon became another Manahune regular.

Irene Hamilton

Margaret and I also spent time in Riccarton with the Hamiltons, and when it was time for John to attend Boys' High School, that was where he boarded.

Another of Mum's Fendall aunts had married Hermann Osmers, and lived at Ross on the West Coast. Their granddaughter Joan attended Girls' High School in Christchurch and would go to stay with the Fisher family for long weekends. She came with her second cousin Audrey to stay at Manahune, and immediately joined the Clan.

Joan Osmers

When Audrey was older, she brought her successive boyfriends to stay, and Irene brought one or two as well.

After the glacier holiday, a few extras arrived at Manahune and joined the throng. At times there would be up to eighteen people sleeping over. When all the beds were full, the surplus lined up on mattresses on the floor in the hall. Everybody joined in with dishes and other necessary chores.

Sometimes the washer would complain about the number of dishes, only to find that for some time, the newly washed dishes had been recycled back to the sink.

Sheep

Above all, Manahune was a sheep farm. I think that in the 1930s there were about 800 Corriedales, and later there were some Southdown rams.

For quite a few years Dad and Uncle shore their own sheep, with a team of home-reared shed hands and wool handlers to help them.

With no electricity, the sheep were blade shorn, and a day's shearing would begin with the blades being sharpened on the hand-turned grind-stone and then given a final honing with an oilstone.

In the week before shearing, the shearing floor would have been swept and scrubbed, the wool bins emptied, and the area round the press cleared for action.

Dad and Margaret would usually do the mustering, and the shed would be filled in the evening, so the wool would be dry next day.

We would wait to pounce on a belly fleece as soon as it touched the floor and, at a very early age, could gather up, and throw a fleece on to the wool table.

A pint-sized Bert would wield the broom, and Margaret and I skirted the fleece and rolled and stored it in the appropriate bin.

Margaret and Bert filled pens while I kept the shearing floor clear.

In those days, the newly shorn sheep were branded before being counted out of the pen, and a spattering of red and black branding fluid was the final embellishment on our shearing clothes.

Dad and Margaret

After a few years Margaret, Bert and I could manage the pressing as well, and leave the men to get on with the shearing.

Mum would prepare large jars of oatmeal water for the shearers. Fine oatmeal, salt and sugar in water, helped them rehydrate and keep up their energy.

Mum and Dorothy took turns supplying morning and afternoon teas to the woolshed.

We would walk back to the house for breakfast and lunch and of course in the evening.

I remember walking up a dewy track at breakfast time, towards a gum tree covered in flowers and suddenly thinking, the cherries must be getting ripe!

Sometimes over shearing time Mum would do all the milking, at times up to 24 cows, alone.

Dipping made its presence known with a permeating smell. It wafted across the creek and filtered through the pines to the house.

If we were not already there, it was time to go and help.

The plunge dip was on the southeast side of the sheep yards. It was an approximate oval in shape, and had a ramp with cross slats on it, leading up to two slightly sloped, concrete drainage pens. To the southeast of the dip, there was a platform that would tip when a lever was pulled. A ramp led to the platform, and on the other side was a small pen with a decoy sheep in it.

The mob of sheep was driven along a long race, up the ramp and, with a bit of encouragement, onto the wet slippery platform. The lever was pulled, and the dip was filled with swimming sheep.

To add insult to injury, the head of each was dunked under that smelly surface, with the pressure of a dipping crook on the back of the neck. Then the crooks were used to assist the sheep to the ramp, and up to the drainage pen.

Bert

The surplus fluid ran back from the pens to the dip. After all the other sheep had had their turn, the decoy was dipped. Finally, the dogs, which had been working hard all day, suddenly found themselves unceremoniously, swimming in the dip.

September heralded Dad's and Uncle's birthdays (both on the fourth), an orchard full of daffodils, and lambing time on Manahune.

In the early days both men would do a beat round the lambing paddocks – Dad always on his pony, and Uncle often on foot, with a chaff sack slung across his shoulder, in case a cold or orphan lamb needed assistance. These lambs would be popped into the sack and carried home.

On a cold wet day, mum would have empty boxes ready with sacks and old woollies in them. She also made sure the fire wasn't burning too fiercely.

On a bad day, up to a dozen lambs might be recuperating in a warm kitchen, and a desperate case could well be lying on a sack in the oven, with the door open.

If the lambs were merely cold, their mums were caught too, and had their feet tied together with binder twine, until they could be transported back to the house yard. Dad would carry one ewe, or even two, in front of him on the pony, but any more than that needed to be collected with the sledge. Potential mums for orphans were also collected.

Bottles of milk completed the décor in the kitchen.

There was a pen on the lawn for mis-mothered lambs, and sometimes there were quite a few to be fed. Dad usually managed to get them mothered off, or gave an odd one away. Margaret raised one to maturity, and it was always her pet.

Tailing was a bloody business.

Ear marking – two holes punched in one ear, and a back bit taken out of the other – could produce a fine spurt of blood onto the face and clothes of the holder.

The actual tailing, with sharpened tailing knife, could do the same for the tailer.

The catchers, us, usually remained bloodless, but still needed a good scrub up at the end of the day.

When the lambs were fat and had been draughted out from the flock; they still had to be driven to Waipara, to the sheep yards by the end of the foot overbridge, on the northwest side of the railway tracks.

Pre-ordered sheep wagons were waiting on the siding, and one would push a wagon in front of the loading ramp, put on the brake, and open the sliding door, before one could start loading.

Dad and Margaret were the drovers, both to Waipara, and also to the Amberley ewe fair. The sale yards were at the north end of Amberley, adjacent to the railway lines.

At ewe fair time, with everybody trying to get their sheep to the fair; the road had many mobs of sheep at fairly close spacing. It was difficult to prevent the sheep from breaking away and boxing with another mob, especially as other traffic was trying to use the road at the same time.

On a few occasions I helped with the droving to Waipara.

Dad, Bert, John, Harold, Margaret, Alice

Mutton was our main source of protein. There was a small mob of sheep in a handy paddock, and once a week Dad would catch one of them.

The actual killing was done on the side lawn near the dairy. I would appear on the scene when the dead sheep had been hoisted in the air, and would assist with the skinning. One soon learned a lot about anatomy. The liver was always taken straight to the kitchen, and Mum was an expert at cooking it.

The carcass was swathed in mutton cloth, and left hanging high overnight, out of reach of marauding animals, and protected from flies. Next day it was cut into joints. In the winter one could keep it hanging for a few days, but in summer with no refrigeration, it was necessary to cook all of it, as soon as possible.

When the weather was hot, we had mutton three times a day. First hot roasts and chops, then cold meat meals for as long as it lasted, with some shepherd's pies along the way.

For most of the year mint was available for mint sauce, and horseradish grew by the fence in the orchard. Mum also made very tasty tomato sauce, chutney and relish.

Soap

Whenever a joint of mutton was roasted, the fat was tipped into a pie-dish before the drippings were made into gravy. The cooled fat was added to a container with the raw kidney fat, which sat in the meat safe, on the back wall of the pantry.

When sufficient fat had accumulated, it was rendered. The kidney fat was placed in a large dish in the oven of the coal range. The melted fat was tipped off and put in the copper in the washhouse.

The fibrous pieces remaining, and the fat from the roasts, went into a stew pan about a quarter full of water. This was brought to the boil, and then cooled. Any impurities stayed in the water, and the solidified fat could be lifted off.

This fat also went into the copper and a small fire was lit to just melt the fat. A measured amount of caustic soda was dissolved in cold water, and stirred into the fat with a long stick. This brew would bubble up, and we were never allowed in the washhouse when Mum was making soap.

When it was thoroughly mixed, the copper was covered, and it was left until next day to set.

I don't remember the technique for removing the soap from the copper, but suspect that something was set into the liquid soap, to lift it out with.

I do remember it being cut into bars with a very large knife on a wooden chopping board. The bars of soap were stored in a box in the washhouse.

About a one-inch slice was cut from the end of a bar, to go in the soap shaker – a wire basket arrangement with a wire handle. The soap shaker was placed in the sink under the hot tap, when one did the dishes. It was then shaken vigorously in the dishwater until sufficient suds appeared. The shaker hung from a nail above the sink.

It was not necessary to clean the copper after soap making, as it was just a flying start for next washday.

On one occasion Mum added citronella to some of the liquid soap, to see how it would be as toilet soap. Nobody appeared to be very impressed, and we reverted to our usual range of toilet soaps; Lux, Lifebuoy, and Solvol for very stained hands.

For baby washing and blankets there were Lux Flakes, and for scrubbing benches and steps we used sandsoap.

To speed up the dissolving of the soap on washdays, the gratings could be covered with water in a container on the stove and then used as soft soap.

Toys

On the back verandah, beside the hall door, was a lidded box that contained our toys. Occasionally we would delve into the box and play with them for a while. There was an assortment of dolls, rather battered, and a gollywog or two, plus some dolls' clothes and china tea seats, a tin sand bucket and wooden spade, and a few miscellaneous bits and pieces that had caught our attention.

Balls came and went over the years, and there were a variety of tops to spin, painted tin humming tops, with holes in the sides and a wind-up mechanism; and shaped, painted wooden ones, activated by winding a piece of string around them, and flicking them to the ground.

Our real interests were further afield. Parked under a pine tree was an old derelict reaper and binder. If one persevered with fingers and a large stone, one could sometimes loosen and remove a bolt, or even something larger. This could occupy an hour or more before we moved on to the treasure trove opposite.

Bert, and Lila, with Alice and Margaret

Here, among an assortment of old tins and broken crockery, one might occasionally glean a small patterned piece of crockery that was gleefully souvenired.

Closer to home there was a pile of apple boxes, behind the coal bin, waiting to be cut into kindling. Some diligent work, with or without a hammer, could dismantle these, and the nails were carefully collected and placed in a tin on Dad's work bench, Dad always saved and straightened every nail that he found, and we could soon do this too.

When we were older an occasional visit was made to the loft in the woolshed. An old tin trunk always made an interesting place to rummage, and some Indian clubs could be experimented with. There was an old pair of crutches too.

To get to the loft one needed to scramble up the pile of full chaff sacks; an exciting exercise in itself.

We owned skipping ropes, both individual, and also a piece of plough line that could be tied to something firm at one end, and swung by a person at the other, for multiple skippers.

John, Harold, Bert

We made kites from newspaper, glued over the edging string with homemade flour and water paste, and spent much time attaching bunches of newspaper sections, along a length of string for a tail. This would inevitably tangle around everything in sight, and we soon learned that lengths of cloth torn from old clothes, and knotted together into one long length, did a much better job.

For many of the kites, the wood we were trying to use was much too heavy; but occasionally we got it right, and some very happy children pressed a part ball of binder twine into service. We were adept at making paper hats and boats from newspaper; and a drop of candle wax in a walnut shell, would support a matchstick mast with paper sail, for sailing on puddle or creek.

Empty cotton reels with a tack, a candle end, a rubber band and a four-inch nail, made wonderful tractors that would climb a gradual slope, and four spaced tacks on the top of a cotton reel made it into a gadget for knitting rats' tails from leftover knitting wool.

Wooden Dolly clothes pegs could have a face drawn on their heads and would be dressed to make attractive little dolls.

Pine cones with two drawing pins for eyes made very realistic owls.

Games of Cowboys and Indians would erupt and take place – under, over, through, around or wherever. Wooden make-believe guns were allowed, but bows and arrows, slings and catapults were not encouraged.

At about Standard 3 or 4 I started playing marbles at school. I must have been reasonably good, because I soon accumulated quite a large bag of assorted marbles, won from lesser players. Probably the only competitive game I was any good at.

Playing knucklebones became fashionable, and I would collect the knucklebone from the dinner joint of mutton, boil it in a small saucepan on the coal range to remove any soft tissue, and add it to my collection.

Some I dyed with permanganate of potash, hoping they would be pink; but they only became brown.

Five knucklebones formed a set, and one would sit on the floor with a set of knucklebones in one's palm, and toss them into the air. The aim was to catch as many as possible on the back of one's hand. There were various sets of moves to be used in finally picking up all the dropped bones. Several people could play, taking turns.

It was easier on the hand if one played on a carpet, so I would retire to the sitting room, to play knucklebones or patience on the carpet there.

All the usual board games, and various card games, helped a cold wet day to pass; but more rowdy games in our large hall, eventuated more frequently.

Homemade stilts, initially 7lb golden syrup tins tied to poles, tested our balance.

The boys had footballs and cricket sets, and quite early they played for the respective clubs.

I attempted to, and Margaret played tennis.

From quite early on we owned a bagatelle set. That was assembled on the extension table in the sitting room. At first Mum feared for the green baize as we wielded the cues, but I don't think it ever suffered major damage.

When I was eight or nine my Grannie gave me a microscope, and it had quite a lot of use.

Margaret, Alice, Bert, John, Harold

The men erected a substantial swing for us on the lawn beside the prunus tree. The prunus was in its infancy, and if we swung high we could just touch its branches with our toes. Much later, there was a swing on the side lawn near the cherry plum.

One of the most memorable toys belonged to Harold. "Diseases" was a fairly small, fawn coloured toy animal, dearly loved and inseparable from Harold. Mum had trouble retrieving it long enough for a much-needed wash, and the name originated from its rather grubby condition.

When the kitchen received its makeover in 1955, and the cylinder cupboard was emptied, Harold was a member of the gang of carpenters on the job. There, in the back corner of the cupboard, warm but just as grubby as always, reclined 'Diseases'.

Tramps

Following the depression, there was a small group of men known as Tramps or 'Swaggies' who would tramp through the countryside with a swag on their back, looking for a few day's work or just a handout, according to their temperament.

They usually had a circuit, and could be expected to turn up about the same time each year. Most were honest but, as always, a few could spoil the reputation of the rest.

Two or three were Manahune regulars and would be given some wood to chop, an evening meal, and a bed in the woolshed. They were usually given some extra food to take with them in the morning.

Trees

Today we are going to top the trees!

Wonderful! We loved topping!

In fact, we loved nearly all the farming jobs; although milking cows could wear a bit thin at times.

At first when the trees were topped, our job was to knock the pinecones off the branches with hammers and put them into sacks. We would also help pile up small branches for a bonfire.

We graduated to trimming side branches off logs with a hatchet and moving bigger branches. Finally we were allowed to cut a small safe branch from a tree ourselves, using a handsaw, and then with a hatchet.

Of course, we had been climbing trees for a lot of our lives and had a good sense of tree safety matters.

In our teens we could do quite a lot of the topping, just leaving the more dangerous tops for the men.

The pine shelterbelts shaded the house and the orchard too much, if left to their own devices. So were topped as required, and the toppings harvested for firewood.

The climax of the day was the bonfire to burn the trimmings. Into the embers went washed potatoes, and an hour or two later, these were eaten by tired, but very happy people.

Uncles and Aunts

The first uncle we knew was Dad's brother Walter, who was a part of our lives until his untimely death in 1944.

Katherine, Dorothy, James, Elizabeth, Selwyn

Mum had a brother, Churchill, who lived in Manaia in Taranaki, with Aunt Joyce and our cousins Dorothy, Selwyn, Elizabeth, Katherine and James. Dorothy and Selwyn wrote regularly to Grannie Fendall while she lived with us. Selwyn visited once while in the armed services during the war.

Aunt Joyce had been a Patterson, and two of her sisters, Rose and Hazel, lived in Canterbury. Rose had married George McLean. Their children were Alec, Jim and Susie. There were occasional visits between our two families.

Hazel was married to Peter Allison. They were both doctors, and lived in Fendalton. When they bought the farm south of Glenbrae, we got to know their family; Tony, Mary, Dick, Bay and Judith. Margaret stayed at their Fendalton home on more than one occasion and I accompanied her once.

Back: Gerald, Elsa, Rilla, Linda; Seated: Hillary, Roger; Front: Nigel, Christopher

Mum's sister Hilda had married Hector King, and they had a small farm with cows, hens, and several large glasshouses of beautiful tomatoes. They lived in Richmond, Nelson, and we were well acquainted with the older children. Their family consisted of Roger, Hillary Elsa, Rilla, Gerald, Nigel, Christopher and Linda. Roger and I, Hilary and Bert, and Elsa and John were the same ages.

Each Christmas cases of apricots were freighted north, and cases of tomatoes were gleefully received in the south.

Bert jnr, Walter, Herbert York, Bert, Alice, Margaret, Jean York, George York

Uncle Hector had two brothers, Les and Prescott. Les and Margaret King with their son Douglas lived on King's Road, in the second-to-last house before the main road. The King parents lived in the original farmhouse. Father King was a keen gardener who loved roses, and his garden was a joy to visit. Prescott and Gladys and their three children, Trevor, Geoffrey and Gwyneth, had a cottage to the west of the main house. We exchanged visits with the King families.

Mum's mother's brothers, Archdeacon George York and the Rev. Herbert York, were incumbent in the parish of St Peter's, Upper Riccarton. They would periodically visit Manahune and christened most of the babies there.

One day Bert came fleeing round the corner of the house to Mum, gasping out, "Two big black wolves!" Very docilely behind him came two tall venerable gentlemen dressed in clerical garb. The Uncles were paying a visit.

Aunt Dorothy, Margaret and I stayed overnight at St Peter's Vicarage before Walter and Dorothy's wedding. Aunt Jean made us very welcome, and I remember a verandah rail covered with beautiful mauve wisteria, and delicious asparagus on toast for breakfast. Margaret and I were the flower girls, and Cousin Roland the best man at that wedding.

On our regular visits to Nelson, we would visit all the York aunts and uncles and, on a later visit to Takaka, Margaret and I were introduced to the Irvine side of the family too.

On the Fendall side of the family, the only aunt I remember meeting was Aunt Ada, who with Uncle Percy Fisher lived in Oxford. When Grannie was with us, we visited Aunt Ada and Uncle Percy.

Vegetables

We always had a large vegetable garden. Sometimes it was in what was known as the lucerne paddock – I do remember an odd lucerne plant by the fence – and sometimes it was up above the pine trees in the homestead paddock. There was a good selection of seasonal vegetables and always a good supply of silver beet, carrots, parsnips and pumpkins to see us through the winter.

We grew our own potatoes, but usually bought onions.

Some turnips would have been drilled with the green feed for the sheep; and when we passed through that paddock, a turnip would be pulled, the soil wiped off with the foliage, and the root peeled and enjoyed. Dad would bring some home for Mum to cook.

Peas would also be drilled on the headland of a paddock and would be much enjoyed raw or cooked. An attempt was made to bottle them, but was unsuccessful. If you have never smelt rotten bottled peas, don't go out of your way to do so!

Cabbages and cauliflowers were sometimes grown and sometimes bought, and we mainly had our own salad vegetables and a good supply of tomatoes and runner beans.

Vehicles

Mum's parents gave Mum and Dad a Model T Ford as a wedding present. Mum could drive and she taught Dad. At least twice they drove it to Nelson to visit Mum's relatives.

The next car was a dark blue Model A Ford, and when Walter married in 1934, this was replaced by two maroon Austins. Walter and Dorothy had the Austin 10 and Dad and Mum had the Austin 7.

That wee Austin was amazing! It carried Mum and Dad and the five of us children wherever we needed to go, to Christchurch, and visits to Oxford relatives, as well as the local running about.

Dad took crates of eggs to Christchurch, and then loaded the wee car up with groceries from Uncle Harold's shop in Madras Street. Sometimes Margaret and I would be with him too.

In 1936 we started going to the Waipara School in the Austin 7. Mum drove us, and initially there were Margaret, Bert and John and the two Quigley children and me. The numbers gradually grew until there were also Noreen O'Carroll, Leila and Mervyn Uren, Bob Dowthwaite, and Mavis Cushion, from the Homestead. There were nine on the back seat; a row of three, three deep. All the children were very patient and never complained at the crowding.

After school, we would all start walking towards home and were usually picked up somewhere near the oak plantation.

During the war, William Henry Reeves came out of retirement to teach at the Wairpara School. He boarded at Quigley's, and we walked the mile to their gate morning and evening, and he took us to school.

At harvest time, Mum would bring lunch for all of us out to the relevant paddock in the Austin 7. She has been known to drive across the slope of a hill with someone standing inside the open front door on the topside, to keep the wheels on the ground.

Sometime in the late 1940s the Austin 7 was painted an orangey brown. It was still being used in 1952.

When Mum was driving to Waipara in the afternoons with an empty car, she said she felt as if the car was flying, as she coasted down the hill opposite the Homestead Lodge.

The only accident I remember was when our cousin Roger drove the Austin 7 to Waipara and tipped it over at the base of the same hill. He suffered a broken forearm and spent a week in hospital.

I don't think the car was damaged too badly.

Wash Day

If the weather was suitable, Monday was usually washday. Sheets and pillowcases would be soaked in the copper overnight. Early next morning, a fire would be lit under the copper, and grated bar soap added. As the water heated, the sheets would be turned over once or twice with the copper stick (an old broom handle). There was a wooden lid on the copper to help it heat more quickly. This was removed when the copper boiled.

Ten minutes or so boiling was usually enough, and then the sheets were carefully lifted out of the copper with the copper stick, into the adjacent wooden tub, which had been three-quarter filled with cold water. The second tub also had cold water in it, in which a blue bag had been soaking until the water was well coloured.

Each sheet was rinsed in the first tub and then a corner was caught up and fed between the rubber rollers of the wringer that sat between the two tubs. The wringer was turned by hand. When the sheets had been well blued, a wooden lid was put over the first tub and the sheets went back through the wringer, and into a metal baby bath that was dual purpose.

The next load in the copper was towels and cotton undies, followed by boil-proof coloureds, and lastly the men's work clothes.

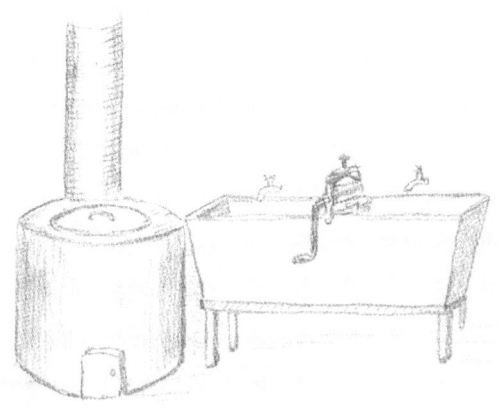

Any badly soiled garments received extra attention with soap and scrubbing brush, on the corrugated wooden washboard.

Woollens were hand-washed with Lux Flakes, and baby washing was always done separately. Soiled nappies were scrubbed and soaked in cold water. All the naps were boiled daily with Lux Flakes in a kerosene tin on the coal range.

Whenever possible Dad would turn the wringer handle on washdays, as it was very heavy work. Then he would carry the wet clothes to the clothesline and help peg them out.

The clothesline ran the full length of the east end of the orchard sufficiently far from the fence to prevent corners of clothing being sampled by inquisitive cows. There was a tall post at each end, and one in the middle; and a clothes prop, with a groove in the top, was attached to the line with lacing wire, in the middle of each section.

Often there would be surplus garments, which were hung on the fence – in the absence of animals – or draped over the currant bushes.

Tablecloths, aprons and cotton dresses were starched. Washing starch was mixed with cold water in a bowl, and then boiling water was stirred in until the starch became translucent. The clothes were dipped into the starch, then hand wrung out. Tablecloths were pulled diagonally, two ways, between two people, to square them; then they were folded in half before being pegged to the line.

If it wasn't blowing too hard, sheets and towels were always folded as they were taken off the line.

Flat irons always sat on the back of the coal range, and a spring-loaded handle clipped into the top for use. The kitchen table was close to the stove. It would be covered with four layers of old blanket topped by an ironing sheet.

If the washing had become too dry, it would be sprinkled with water, folded and rolled up together, then put aside while the rest of the ironing was done.

There was an iron-shaped metal stand on the table, to put the iron on if necessary, also, there was a folded cloth to wipe the sole of the iron on, when it first came off the stove.

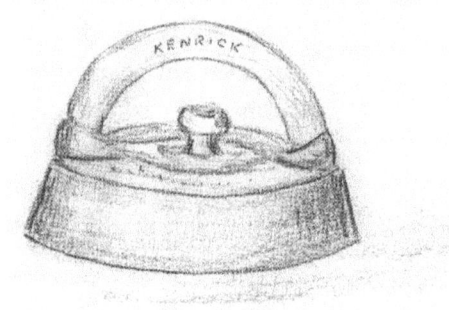

One would become very adept at judging the heat of the iron, with a very, very, quick tap on the sole. As the iron cooled, one would iron something suited to that temperature, before replacing that iron on the stovetop and clipping onto the next one.

Flat irons were quite heavy, and it was hot work ironing beside the hot stove. Woollens, and particularly serge skirts and trousers, were covered by a damp cloth, or sheet of brown paper, for ironing, to prevent them becoming shiny.

Water

"Water is precious!"
'One does not waste water!"

When the storage capacity for clean water, for a household of four adults and three young children, was 1,200 gallons, and the Waipara rainfall is so variable, every drop of water was valuable.

"Just wet your tooth brush then turn off the tap."

"Only about 4 inches of water in the bath, and all of you take it in turns for that bath, with a little extra hot added for the last person."

"Don't use the inside flush toilet."

"Only a little water in the hand basin and turn the tap off."

"Wash the dishes in a bowl and empty the water onto the garden."

"Wash vegetables in a bowl."

"Peel potatoes dry, then rinse them in the bowl."

The runoff from the roof of the main house was collected in two 400-gallon tanks on a tank stand, and the water piped to the hot water cylinder, and the cold taps in the house.

The runoff from the lean-to, filled the 400-gallon rainwater tank, on a lower stand, and was accessed by a tap on the tank.

We were all adept at tapping the side of a tank, and telling by sound how many rungs of water were in it. If a drought continued too long, the creek water was sometimes pumped into the two main tanks, so the wetback that heated the water cylinder didn't run dry.

This was very necessary, as the coal range was our only means of cooking, so was nearly always alight.

The rainwater tank must never be contaminated, as it must be available for drinking and rinsing milk buckets.

Some years it was necessary to dig out the spring, beneath the hill at the back of the front swamp. The water was collected in cream cans and filtered through an unglazed earthenware filter before being used. As a drink it was bitter; rainwater tasted sweet after it.

When the separator shed was built by the cowshed, a rainwater tank was installed beside it, and the runoff from the cowshed roof was collected to be used at the cowshed.

Sometimes, when there was plenty of rain, the tanks would overflow; so an extra 600-gallon tank was added to the main storage area.

At some stage after Walter's house was built, it was decided to build a large concrete, underground water storage tank at each house. Now there was virtually no wastage of beautiful rainwater, and the stored water was hand pumped to replenish the main tanks.

The value of a shower of rain was assessed by how many rungs of water were added to the rainwater tank.

Dad had a rain gauge, and always kept records of the rainfall. He accumulated quite a pile of notebooks with these recordings.

Unless it was too cold, or too prolonged, we loved rain. On went the gumboots, coats and oilskin hats, and out we went to play in the yard, usually stick in hand, to drag between puddles, and to encourage the little rivulets that finally joined and ran down beside the track to the creek.

When it was a really good rainfall, this would be happening in all the gullies, until finally the creek was in flood.

The creek was out of bounds when we were small; and when we were bigger, we were not allowed near a flooded creek, unless Dad was with us.

A few yards upstream from the ford there was a small waterfall. Each flood would cause the waterfall to cut back a few feet or a few yards. Usually there would be a small pond remaining at the foot of the fall, its size depending on the terrain it was cutting through.

Upstream the creek meandered, first through a fairly large swamp area and then, en route to the waterfall, it passed through two reasonable sized pools. We treated these pools with respect, and gave them a wide berth as we passed by.

For some years the waterfall did not recede very much, but later its progress was measured by chains as it cut back and drained the two pools, and finally, very quickly, the swamp.

After each flood there were two points of interest. How far had the waterfall receded? And, had any more moa bones been found?

Dad's collection of moa bones increased year by year; it included some good thigh and toe bones, plus a skull, and a whole drawer full of miscellaneous bits and pieces. Periodically they were laid out on the lawn to see how much of a skeleton had accumulated.

To raise water from the creek for use in the orchard and garden, a ram pump had been installed in the creek, where the gorge area began. An area of creek bed was dug out slightly to the side, and the domes and working parts of the ram were set up there. An inlet pipe ran from a pool below the ford.

After a small eel had found its way down that pipe and blocked the ram, Dad covered the inlet with a tin can, with holes punched in its base. A pipe came from the ram, up the hill to near the corner of the house, and a hose led the water to wherever it was required.

After Walter's house was built, there was a tap at the ram, to direct the water to either house, but only one at a time.

The time came to upgrade the ford. Three large concrete pipes – we could almost stand up in them as they lay on their sides – were set in the creek bed, and the track on either side was extended with rocks and concrete, and topped with shingle.

This made a wonderful culvert, and crossing the creek with vehicles (motorised or horse drawn) was now a breeze.

That winter there was a flood.

The water, dammed up by the culvert, spread until it covered the entire front swamp area. Manahune now had a lake, but not for long. The weight of the water finally swept away the culvert, which was, of necessity, replaced by a bridge.

Although the approaches have occasionally suffered some flood damage, the bridge has done valiantly ever since.

Wild Flowers

Tiny blue forget-me-nots and white violets with tiny purple markings (and no smell), grew in the swamp below the woolshed, and raupo flourished too. Also in that region was a very sweet-smelling grass. In the swamp and around the creek were the yellow buttons of castoroil plant - pretty, but a revolting smell - yellow trefoil, assorted buttercups, dandelions and toi toi.

On the bank behind was the cabbage tree, and later, a self-seeded gooseberry, that was very prolific.

Below that, grew some *muehlenbeckia* bushes. There was a patch of bracken and plenty of matagouri (with its tiny, sweet-smelling white flowers). A lone tawhini grew there too, and further along some tutu.

At the end of the woolshed flat (past the cabbage tree) by the top of the downhill track, there was a very nice *pimelia prostrata* with tiny grey leaves and white flowers.

Over by the ram-pump was a patch of mint, probably planted by Dad, and usually there was enough watercress to have in Marmite sandwiches.

On the nor'west facing bank (above the creek, downstream from the ram), grew a tiny stiff-leaved native, with edible orange berries the size of sweet pea seeds – *patotara*, and patches of biddy-biddy – *acaena glabra*.

Among the tussock areas there were wild Spaniard *aciphylla collensoi* and blue and white harebells *walenbergia*, and sometimes on the nor'west facing side of a gully, would be the odd white gentian.

Among the rocks were a few patches of alpine hard fern *Blechmum penna-marina-alpina*, and odd plants of black shield fern.

Clumps of blanket weed *mullein*, with their spires of yellow flowers, were quite plentiful.

In the summer, ponds and still areas in the creek had a good covering of *kareaea azolla filiculoides*. We certainly didn't know its name; 'pond weed' did us.

In the grass on the road verges, there were numerous little red, pink and white flowers. Their leaves and stalks were covered with fine hairs that made them feel slightly sticky.

Opposite the Shellrock road was a patch of chicory, and we loved its bright blue flowers. There were also stalky grey-leafed plants with flowers like smallish mauve cornflowers.

One or two patches of Californian thistles made their presence felt, as we endeavoured to remove the almost invisible prickles from our fingers at harvest time.

The Scotch thistles were not so sneaky, and they provided a bonus. By carefully grasping the purple flower filaments and pulling outwards and down, a flower can be gathered. Now, starting just above the stalk, each prickle is carefully peeled off, row by row.

Soon all the prickles are gone and the flower parts can be pulled off the basal disc. It makes a pleasant nutty snack, almost worth the effort of obtaining it.

Xmas Trees

Mum and Dad took two tiny girls to the spare room beside the bathroom. They opened the door and took us in. There was an amazing sight. A huge pine tree had grown up in the middle of the room.

Alice, Heather, Bert, Joan, Margaret, Derek, John

It reached to the ceiling and appeared to fill the room. It was pretty and it sparkled; there were bright coloured things growing on the branches. My first Christmas tree!

Dorothy and Mum had decorated another tree that I clearly remember.

The Quigley children and all the Manahune children had a Christmas party on the lawn beside the young wattle tree, which had been beautifully decorated all over.

Yeast

Sitting on a high shelf in the pantry was an oldish cardboard packet. Occasionally some flakes from its contents would drift onto the shelf. It was labelled 'Hops'.

At some stage Mum made a mixture with potato and hops, and I don't know what else. She had found a recipe for yeast. I have no idea how successful this was, but it was not repeated. Probably it was easier, and less effort and mess, to just buy a cake of compressed yeast from the grocer.

There was always yeast in the house, and Mum's bread and buns were legendary.

Ginger beer came and went in cycles. At times the recipe included yeast; and at times someone would give Mum a ginger beer bug, which needed daily attention. Of course, this bug was a yeast as well.

Young People's Club

After the war there were a lot of teenagers in the district, and the Waipara Young People's Club was formed.

We met one night a week in the Waipara hall, and had a good range of activities, including table tennis.

An active committee organised hikes and, before I left the district, a weekend camp was held at Lake Taylor.

333

Harold was full of energy and bounce as he strived to compete with his older siblings. This took its toll on an eight-year-old, and there came the day when Harold crashed.

As two brothers, and two future brothers-in-law, had a rough and tumble all around and over his bed, Harold slept peacefully on.

What is the difference between a weasel and a stoat?

Well, a weasel is weasily distinguished, because a stoat is stoatally different.

Glossary

Barbed wire outrigger: a single strand of barbed wire running parallel to a fence, to protect the fence from the horses.

Cavings: the husks of the wheat separated from the grain by the threshing mill. Cavings could be used as a mattress filling, but were pricklier than chaff.

Chaff: Oat straw and grain cut into 1/8-inch lengths by the chaff cutter. Used for feeding horses.

Hames: A metal frame buckled on top of the padded leather horse collar. It had a swivelled hook each side for attaching the chains from an implement. The top knobbed ends extended above the collar, and were used for carrying coiled ropes, lunch bags, etc.

Long drop: A deep hole dug in the ground, with mobile toilet building placed over the top.

Pinny: Pinafore.

Slate: A flat smooth plate of fine-grained metamorphic rock, in a wooden frame. The slate pencil was a small rod of soft slate for writing with on the slate. The slate was wiped clean with a damp cloth.

Whare: Small house. Maori

www.ingramcontent.com/pod-product-compliance
Lightning Source LLC
Chambersburg PA
CBHW061656120626
46550CB00003B/966